Nick Vandome

Windows 11

for PCs, laptops and tablets

In easy steps is an imprint of In Easy Steps Limited
16 Hamilton Terrace · Holly Walk · Leamington Spa
Warwickshire · United Kingdom · CV32 4LY
www.ineasysteps.com

Notice of Liability
Every effort has been made to ensure that this book contains accurate
and current information. However, In Easy Steps Limited and the
author shall not be liable for any loss or damage suffered by readers
as a result of any information contained herein.

Trademarks
Microsoft® and Windows® are registered trademarks of Microsoft
Corporation. All other trademarks are acknowledged as belonging to
their respective companies.

In Easy Steps Limited supports The Forest Stewardship Council (FSC),
the leading international forest certification organization. All our titles
that are printed on Greenpeace approved FSC certified paper carry the
FSC logo.

MIX
Paper from
responsible sources
FSC® C020837

Printed and bound in the United Kingdom

ISBN 978-1-84078-947-8

Contents

1 Introducing Windows 11

This chapter shows how to get up and running with Windows 11, including its new features and its interface, keyboard shortcuts, and creating and using a Microsoft Account.

About Windows

Windows is an operating system made by Microsoft, for PCs (personal computers), laptops and tablets. The operating system is the software that organizes and controls all of the components (hardware and software) in your computer.

The first operating system from Microsoft was known as MS-DOS (Microsoft Disk Operating System). This was a non-graphical, line-oriented, command-driven operating system, able to run only one application at a time. The original Windows system was an interface manager that ran on top of the MS-DOS system, providing a graphical user interface (GUI) and using clever processor and memory management to allow it to run more than one application or function at a time.

The basic element of Windows was its "windowing" capability. A window (with a lowercase w) is a rectangular area used to display information or to run a program or app. Several windows can be opened at the same time so that you can work with multiple applications. This provided a dramatic increase in productivity, in comparison with the original MS-DOS.

Between 1985 and 2015 Microsoft released numerous versions of the operating system, each with its own intermediate versions to add updates and security fixes to the operating system. These versions of Windows included Windows 95, Windows XP, Windows 8 and Windows 10 (there was no Windows 9).

Windows 10 has been in operation since 2015; there has been no numerical update to the operating system. Instead of releasing Windows 11, 12, etc., each new version has been given a Windows 10 title – e.g. the Windows 10 Anniversary Update; the Windows 10 Creators Update.

For several years, Microsoft stated that there would not be a full naming update to Windows 10; instead, it would continue with incremental updates, usually on an annual basis. However, nothing stays still in the world of technology and Windows 11 was released in October 2021, recognizing the fact that the operating system required a major update to keep it at the forefront of the evolution of PCs and laptops, and also mobile devices such as the Surface tablet. Windows 11 is a full redesign of the operating system, in terms of its overall appearance, and Microsoft has also taken the opportunity to add a range of new features and functions.

The New icon pictured above indicates a new or enhanced feature introduced with Windows 11.

New Features in Windows 11

Windows 11 is a significant update to its predecessor in terms of look and feel and also has a range of new functionality. However, it retains the features that will be familiar to Windows users, ensuring that Windows 11 is a sleek, efficient, modern operating system for Windows users.

Redesigned interface

The first obvious change with Windows 11 is a cleaner, brighter user interface, starting with the Desktop.

These features are new or updated in Windows 11.

Updated Start button and Start menu

Two of the most important elements of Windows have been redesigned in Windows 11: the Start button, which has always been in the bottom left-hand corner, now takes up a more central position, with the Taskbar centered on the screen rather than stretching all the way across it; and the Start menu has been completely redesigned to make it easier to find apps and files.

The color of the Start menu and the Taskbar below it can be set to Light or Dark. To do this, select **Settings** > **Personalization** > **Colors** and select **Light** or **Dark** in the **Choose your mode** section. The color of the Start menu and the Taskbar are a matter of personal taste (although the Dark option can make items clearer). The majority of the examples in the book use the **Dark** option.

...cont'd

Widgets

The Widgets app is a customizable panel that can be used to display a range of real-time information, such as newsfeeds and weather forecasts.

There are no specific settings for the Widgets app, but there is a **Manage interests** option for determining what appears within the app. This can be accessed from the **Account** button in the top right-hand corner of the Widgets panel.

Microsoft Teams Chat

Microsoft Teams is a collaboration and communication app. The full version is included with Windows 11, pinned to the Taskbar, and there is also a pop-out Teams **Chat** app that can be used independently of the full version, for text, video and audio chats.

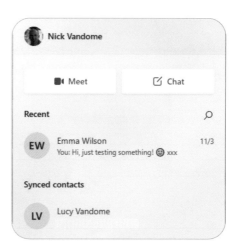

Android apps

Through the Microsoft Store, Android apps can now be used with Windows 11, which means that users of Android smartphones can access some of the same apps as they use on their smartphones. This is done by downloading the apps from the Amazon Appstore, which is also accessed from within the Microsoft Store.

The Android apps feature did not have its full functionality with the initial Windows 11 release, although this will be enhanced with subsequent updates.

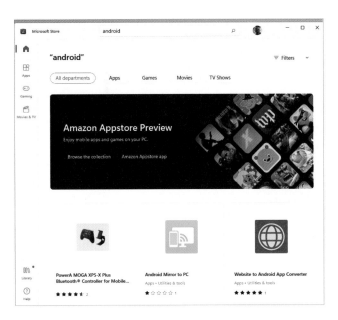

Snap Layouts

Some previous versions, including Windows 10, had options for displaying and managing multiple apps within a single screen, known as Snap Layouts. This has been refined in Windows 11 so that the layouts can be accessed from the control buttons at the top of each app, based on pre-designed templates.

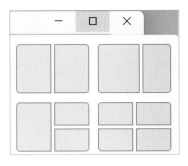

Obtaining Windows 11

Windows 11 is an online service, rather than just a stand-alone operating system. This means that by default, Windows 11 is obtained and downloaded online, with subsequent updates and upgrades also provided online on a regular basis.

The main ways of installing Windows 11 are:

- **Use Windows Update** – Replace an older version of Windows, retaining the installed applications and settings. This can be done through the **Settings** app (select **Windows Update** and click on the **Check for updates** button).

- **Microsoft website** – Visit the software download page on the Microsoft website (**microsoft.com/en-us/software-download/windows11**) to use the **Windows 11 Installation Assistant** to download Windows 11.

For more information about the Settings app, see pages 42-57.

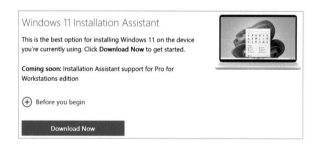

- **Pre-installed** – Buy a new PC or laptop with Windows 11 already installed.

Some of the steps that the installation will go through are:

- **Personalize**. These are settings that will be applied to your version of Windows 11. These settings can also be selected within the Settings app once Windows 11 has been installed.

- **Settings**. You can choose to have express settings applied or customize them.

- **Microsoft Account**. You can set up a Microsoft Account during installation, or once you have started Windows 11.

- **Privacy**. Certain privacy settings can be applied during the setup process for Windows 11.

Keyboard Shortcuts

As you become more confident using Windows 11, you may want to access certain items more quickly. There are a range of keyboard shortcuts that can be used to access some of the items you use most frequently.

The majority of the shortcuts are accessed together with the WinKey (Windows key) on the keyboard. To use the keyboard shortcuts, press:

- **WinKey** to access the Start menu at any time.

- **WinKey** + **L** to lock the computer and display the Lock screen.

- **WinKey** + **I** to access the Settings app.

- **WinKey** + **K** to connect new devices.

- **WinKey** + **Q** to access the Search window.

- **WinKey** + **D** to access the Desktop.

- **WinKey** + **M** to access the Desktop with the active window minimized.

- **WinKey** + **E** to access File Explorer, displaying the Quick access section.

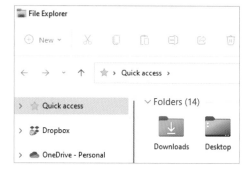

- **WinKey** + **T** to display thumbnails on the Desktop Taskbar.

- **WinKey** + **U** to access the Accessibility options in the Settings app.

- **WinKey** + **X** to access the Power User menu, which gives you quick access to items including the Desktop and File Explorer.

- **Alt** + **F4** to close a Windows 11 app.

- **Ctrl** + **Shift** + **Esc** to access Task Manager.

The options on the Power User menu are also known as the administration tools.

Windows 11 for Touch

One of the aims of Windows 11 is to make the operating system familiar to users with a keyboard and mouse. For touchscreen devices such as tablets and laptops with precision touchpads, the same overall operation of Windows 11 has been maintained so that users can feel comfortable with the operating system regardless of the device on which they are using it.

Continuum

Continuum refers to the function of Windows 11 where you can start something on one Windows 11 device and then continue working on it on another. For instance, you could start a letter in Word on a desktop computer, save it, and then pick up where you left off on the Microsoft tablet, Surface. Continuum works between desktop computers, laptops and tablets.

Using touch

Touchscreen devices and those with precision touchpads can be used with Windows 11 to navigate through a number of gestures, swipes and taps on the screen or touchpad. Some of the gestures that can be used with touchscreen or touchpad devices using Windows 11 are:

- Swipe inward from the right-hand edge to access the Notifications area.

- Swipe inward from the left-hand edge to access Task View for currently open apps, and the Timeline.

- In an open Windows 11 app, swipe downward from the top of the screen to access the app's toolbar.

- In an open Windows 11 app, use a long swipe downward from the top of the screen to close the app.

- Swipe upward from the bottom of the screen to access the Taskbar (when an app is at full screen).

- Tap with three fingers on a touchpad to bring up the personal digital assistant, Cortana.

Hot tip

Aside from the gestures used on a touchscreen device, much of the operation of Windows 11 has been consolidated between computers with a mouse and keyboard, and mobile devices.

Control Panel and Categories

In previous versions of Windows, the Control Panel played an important role in applying settings for a number of different functions. Because of this, it could be accessed in several different ways. However, in Windows 11, more of the Control Panel functionality has been moved to the Settings app, and there are less obvious methods for accessing the Control Panel. Despite this, it can still be used to access a variety of settings.

1. Click on the **Start** button to bring up the **Start** menu for accessing apps

2. Click **All apps** and then click on the **Windows Tools** button

3. Click on the **Control Panel** button

4. Click on the **Control Panel** categories to view the content within them

5. Click here to access options for viewing the Control Panel layout

6. The icons views display a wider range of options from within the Control Panel than Category view

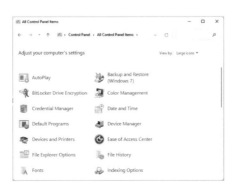

For more information about the Start menu and the Start button, see pages 22-29.

More functions from the Control Panel are being migrated to the Settings app with each new version of Windows 11. However, some remain in the Control Panel and will be opened here, even if the link to it is physically located in the Settings app.

If you still use the Control Panel regularly, pin it to either the Start menu or the Taskbar, or both. For details about pinning items, see pages 77-78.

Using a Microsoft Account

We live in a world of ever-increasing computer connectivity, where users expect to be able to access their content wherever they are and share it with their friends and family in a variety of ways, whether it is by email, messaging or photo sharing. This is known as cloud computing, with content being stored on online servers, from where it can be accessed by authorized users.

In Windows 11, this type of connectivity is achieved with a Microsoft Account. This is a registration system (which can be set up with most email addresses and a password) that provides access to a number of services via the Windows 11 apps. These include:

Beware

Without a Microsoft Account you will not be able to access the full functionality of the apps listed here.

- **Mail**. This is the Windows 11 email app that can be used to access and manage your different email accounts.

- **Teams**. This is the collaboration and communication app.

- **People**. This is the address book app, accessed from the Mail app (above).

- **Calendar**. This is the calendar and organizer app.

- **Microsoft Store**. This is the online store for previewing and downloading additional apps.

- **OneDrive**. This is the online backup and sharing service.

Creating a Microsoft Account

It is free to create a Microsoft Account. This can be done with an email address and, together with a password, provides a unique identifier for logging in to your Microsoft Account and related apps. There are several ways in which you can create and set up a Microsoft Account:

- During the initial setup process when you install Windows 11. You will be asked if you want to create a Microsoft Account at this point. If you do not, you can always do so at a later time.

- When you first open an app that requires access to a Microsoft Account. When you do this, you will be prompted to create a new account.

- From the **Accounts** section of the **Settings** app (see page 49).

...cont'd

Whichever way you use to create a Microsoft Account, the process is similar.

1 When you are first prompted to sign in with a Microsoft Account you can enter your account details, if you have one; or

2 Click on the **No account? Create one!** link

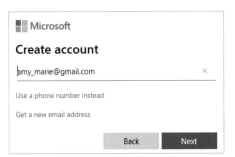

3 Enter your name, an email address and a password (on the next screen) for your Microsoft Account

Hot tip

Microsoft Account details can also be used as your sign-in for Windows 11 (see pages 19-20).

4 Click on the **Next** button to move through the registration process

5 A verification code is required to finish setting up the Microsoft Account. This will be sent to the email address entered in Step 3. Click on the **Next** button to complete the Microsoft Account setup

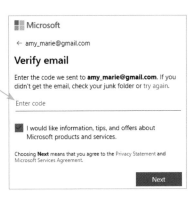

Sign-in Options

Each time you start up your computer using Windows 11 with a Microsoft Account, you will need to sign in. This is a security feature so that no-one can gain unauthorized access to your account on your computer. The sign-in process starts with the Lock screen and then you have to enter your sign-in details.

1 When you start your computer, the Lock screen will be showing. This is linked to the sign-in screen

2 Click on the **Lock screen** or press any key to move to the sign-in screen. Enter your sign-in details and press **Enter** on your keyboard

3 On the sign-in screen, click on this button to select **Accessibility** options

4 On the sign-in screen, click on this button to select **Power off** options including **Shut down**, **Sleep** and **Restart**

For details about personalizing the Lock screen, see page 47.

You can lock your PC at any time by pressing **WinKey** + **L**.

You will get an error message if you enter the wrong password or if you simply mis-key and cause an incorrect character to be added.

If you forget your PIN for your Microsoft Account, click on the **I forgot my PIN** link on the sign-in screen to reset it.

5 If there are other users with an account on the same computer, their names will be displayed here

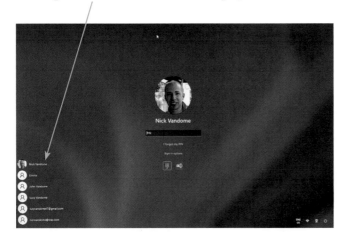

6 Click on another user to access their own sign-in screen

Sign-in settings

Settings for how you sign in can be accessed from the Accounts section in the Settings app.

1 Access the **Settings** app and click on the **Accounts** button

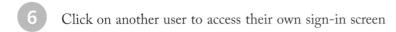

2 Under **Sign-in options**, select options for how you sign in from the Lock screen

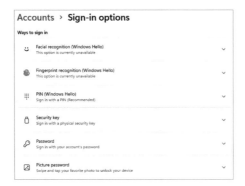

You can sign in with a Local account or a Microsoft Account. If you sign in with the latter, you will have access to related services, such as Mail and People. Also, you will be able to sync your settings and use them on another computer when you log in with your account.

For details about using the Settings app, see pages 42-57.

Facial recognition and **Fingerprint recognition** are functions that use biometric authentication for signing in to Windows 11. This is either done by scanning your face or with a fingerprint reader. However, specialist hardware is required for this to operate.

...cont'd

Using a PIN to sign in

Using a PIN to sign in to your Windows 11 computer can be a more convenient option than remembering a long password each time (although a password still has to be used when an account is created). To use a PIN to sign in:

1 Access the **Sign-in options** section of the Settings app, as shown on page 19, and click on the **PIN (Windows Hello)** option

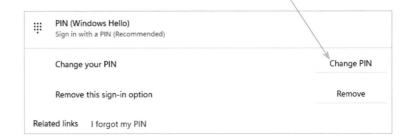

2 Click on the **Change PIN** button to change an existing PIN (or **Add** to create a new one)

⠿ PIN (Windows Hello) Sign in with a PIN (Recommended)		
Change your PIN		Change PIN
Remove this sign-in option		Remove
Related links I forgot my PIN		

20

Don't forget

If you want to create a picture password for signing in, you must have a touchscreen device. Select a picture and draw a pattern to use as your sign-in.

3 Enter the new PIN and enter it again to confirm it. Click on the **OK** button to finish setting up the PIN

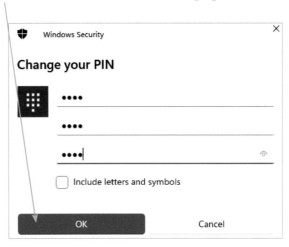

2 Getting Started

This chapter looks at some of the main features of Windows 11, focusing on the Start menu, using the Desktop and the Taskbar, and Task View. It also covers using widgets for news and weather updates, the personal digital assistant, Cortana, for voice searching over your computer for a range of items, and switching between users on your computer.

The Start Button

The Start button has been a significant part of Windows computing for numerous versions of the operating system. There have been various changes to the Start button over the years and it has again been redesigned in Windows 11, with the main difference being that it occupies a more central position on the screen, as opposed to being located in the left-hand corner.

Using the Start button

The Start button provides access to the apps on your Windows 11 computer and also to the enhanced Start menu.

1. Click on the **Start** button at the bottom left-hand side of the Taskbar

2. The **Start** menu is displayed

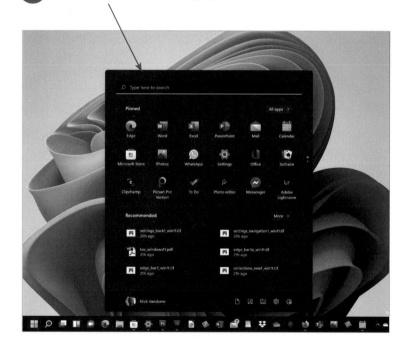

3. The Start menu contains access to all of the apps on your computer, and also recommended items

4. Other items can also be accessed from the Start button by right-clicking on it; see the next page

The Start button has been updated in Windows 11.

Items on the Start menu can be customized from the **Personalization** > **Start** section of the Settings app.

22

Click on the **Power** button on the Start menu to access options for **Sleep**, **Shut down** or **Restart**.

Power User menu

In addition to accessing the Start menu, the Start button also provides access to the Power User menu, which can be accessed as follows:

 Right-click on the **Start** button to view the Power User menu

Apps and Features
Mobility Center
Power Options
Event Viewer
System
Device Manager
Network Connections
Disk Management
Computer Management
Windows Terminal
Windows Terminal (Admin)
Task Manager
Settings
File Explorer
Search
Run
Shut down or sign out   >
Desktop

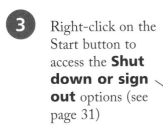 Click on the relevant buttons to view items including the **Desktop** and other popular locations such as **File Explorer**

The Start button Power User menu in Step 1 has a number of options for accessing system functions, such as **Device Manager** and **Disk Management**. The options vary depending on the type of device being used.

23

 Right-click on the Start button to access the **Shut down or sign out** options (see page 31)

Settings   Sign out
File Explorer   Sleep
Search   Update and shut down
Run   Shut down
Shut down or sign out > Update and restart
Desktop   Restart

The Start Menu

The Start menu has been a permanent fixture in Windows, but its appearance and functionality has changed significantly over the years. This evolution continues with Windows 11, with a newly designed Start menu. This is where you can access areas within your computer, perform certain functions, and also access apps from a variety of locations. To use the Start menu:

The Start menu has been updated in Windows 11.

1. Click on the **Start button** to access the **Start menu**. **Pinned** apps (see page 78) are shown at the top of the Start menu, with **Recommended** items below. Click on an item to open it

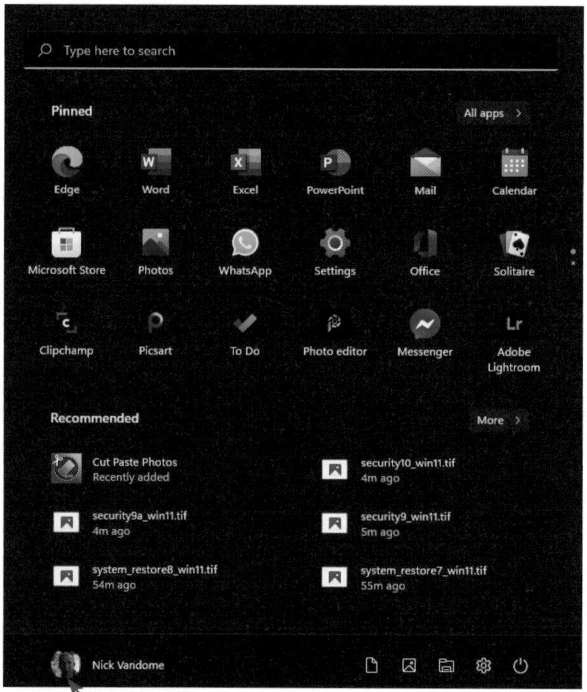

2. Click here to access your own account settings or sign out from your account

3. Click on the **Power** button for options to **Sleep** your computer, **Shut down** or **Restart**

Some of the default items on the bottom toolbar of the Start menu can be customized to a certain extent (see pages 28-29).

The options in Step 3 can also be accessed by right-clicking on the Start button and clicking on the **Shut down or sign out** button.

4 Click on the **All apps** button at the top of the **Pinned** section, to view all of the apps on your computer

Hot tip

Scroll up and down on the **Pinned** section to view more items, or click on these buttons at the right-hand side of the Pinned section:

5 Scroll up and down the **All apps** section to view the available apps. Click on one to open it

25

Don't forget

At the top of the **All apps** window is a list of your **Most used** apps. This changes depending on which apps you use most regularly, if this option is turned **On** as described in Step 4 on page 28.

6 Click on the **Back** button in the top right-hand corner of the All apps panel to go back to the main Start menu

...cont'd

7 On the **All apps** screen, click on one of the alphabetic headings; e.g. B

8 An alphabetic grid is displayed

9 Click on a character on the alphabetic grid to go to the relevant section

Repositioning the Start Button

Although the Start button has moved into a more central position, along with the Taskbar, it is still possible to restore it to the left-hand corner, if desired. This is done by moving the whole of the Taskbar to the left. To do this:

1 Click on the **Settings** app on the Taskbar or the Start menu

Repositioning the Start button is a new feature in Windows 11.

2 Click on the **Personalization** tab

3 Click on the **Taskbar** option

> Taskbar
> Taskbar behaviors, system pins

4 Click on the **Taskbar behaviors** option

> **Taskbar behaviors**
> Taskbar alignment, badging, automatically hide, and multiple displays

All of the icons on the Taskbar are aligned to the left, in addition to the **Start** button, if you choose this option.

5 Click here in the **Taskbar alignment** panel to select options for how the Taskbar is aligned

6 Click on the **Left** option to align the Taskbar to the left-hand side, situating the Start button in the left-hand corner

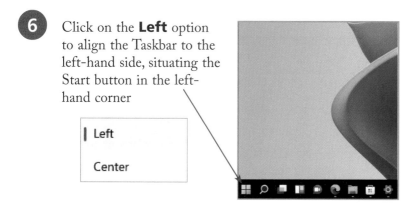

Customizing the Start Menu

Windows 11 is very adaptable and can be customized in several ways so that it works best for you. This includes the Start menu, which can be set to behave in certain ways and have specific items added to it. To do this:

1 Click on the **Settings** app on the Taskbar

2 Click on the **Personalization** tab

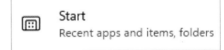

3 Click on the **Start** option

	Start
	Recent apps and items, folders

4 Under **Start**, select whether to show recently added apps, show most used apps, or show recently opened items on the Start menu

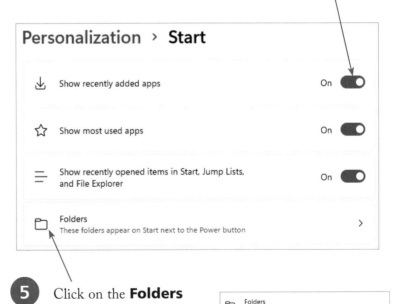

5 Click on the **Folders** option to select items that appear on the Start menu

Folders
These folders appear on Start next to the Power button

Don't forget

Recently added and most used apps appear at the top of the **All apps** section of the Start menu, if these options are turned **On**.

6 Drag the buttons **On** for items you want to appear on the Start menu; e.g. File Explorer, the Settings app, the Documents Library, and the Pictures app

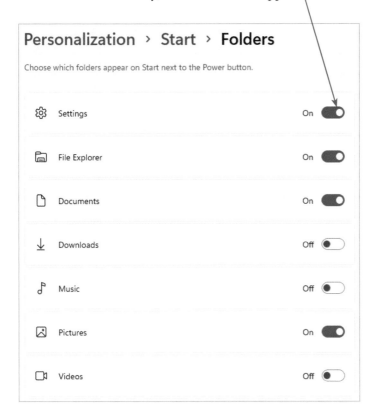

Personalization > Start > **Folders**

Choose which folders appear on Start next to the Power button.

⚙ Settings	On	⬤
🗁 File Explorer	On	⬤
🗋 Documents	On	⬤
↓ Downloads	Off	◯
𝄞 Music	Off	◯
🖼 Pictures	On	⬤
🎥 Videos	Off	◯

If you find that you do not use some items very much once they have been added to the Start menu, they can be removed by dragging their buttons **Off** in Step 6.

7 Items selected in Step 6 appear on the Start menu, next to the **Power** button

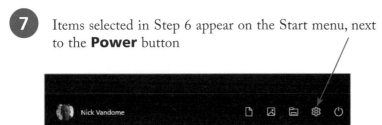

Nick Vandome

The Desktop and Taskbar

The Desktop is an integral part of Windows, and when you turn on Windows 11 it opens at the Desktop. This also displays the Taskbar at the bottom of the screen:

The Desktop can also be accessed by pressing **WinKey** + **D** or by right-clicking on the Start button and selecting **Desktop**.

Hot tip

Move the cursor over the bottom right-hand corner of the screen and click on **Show desktop** to display the Desktop at any time.

Shortcut icons   Desktop background

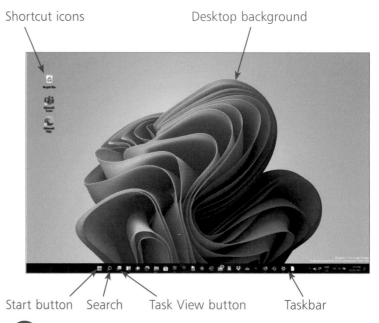

Start button   Search   Task View button   Taskbar

1 Move the cursor over items on the Taskbar to see open windows for that item. Click on a window to make that the active one

2 The Notifications area at the right-hand side of the Taskbar has speaker, network and other system tools. Click on one to see more information about that item

Don't forget

If an app has two or more windows open, each of them will be displayed when you move the cursor over the app's icon on the Taskbar.

30

Shutting Down

Options for shutting down Windows have been amended with some versions of the operating system. In Windows 11, this functionality can be accessed from the Start menu.

Shutting down from the Start menu

1 Click on the **Start** button

2 Click on the **Power** button

3 Click on either the **Sleep**, **Shut down** or **Restart** buttons; or

Hot tip

For some updates to Windows, you will need to restart your computer for them to take effect.

4 Right-click on the **Start** button and select either **Sign out**, **Sleep**, **Shut down** or **Restart** from the **Shut down or sign out** option

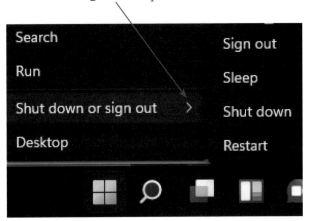

Task View

A useful feature in Windows 11 is the Task View option. This is located on the Taskbar and can be used to view all open apps and also add new Desktops. To use Task View:

1 Click on this button on the Taskbar

2 Task View displays minimized versions of currently open apps and windows

3 As more windows are opened, the format is arranged accordingly

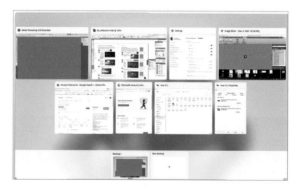

4 If an app has more than one window open (e.g. File Explorer), each window is displayed within Task View

5 Click on a window in Task View to make it the active window

Don't forget

Apps can only be open on one Desktop at a time. So, if an app is open on one Desktop and you try to open it on another, you will be taken to the Desktop with the already open app. For adding Desktops, see the next page.

Don't forget

Although the shortcuts and background are the same for each Desktop, the Taskbar will change depending on the open apps.

Adding Desktops

Another function within Task View is for creating additional Desktops. This can be useful if you want to separate different categories of tasks on your computer. For instance, you may want to keep your open entertainment apps on a different Desktop from your productivity ones. To create additional Desktops:

If you add too many Desktops it may become confusing in terms of the content on each one.

1 Click on the **Task View** button on the Taskbar

2 The current Desktop is displayed

The default names of different Desktops cannot be changed; i.e. they are Desktop 1, Desktop 2, etc.

3 Click on the **New desktop** button

4 The new Desktop is displayed at the top of the Task View window

To delete a Desktop, click on the Task View button and click on the cross that appears when you hover your mouse over the Desktop you want to remove.

5 Click on the new Desktop to access it. Each Desktop has the same background and shortcuts

6 Open apps on the new Desktop. These will be separate from the apps on any other Desktop

Click on the **Task View** button to move between Desktops.

Widgets

The Widgets panel in Windows 11 contains a number of real-time items, such as newsfeeds and weather forecasts, that change as new information becomes available. Items in the Widgets panel are fully customizable. To use the Widgets panel:

The Widgets app is a new feature in Windows 11.

1 Click on this button on the Taskbar

2 The Widgets panel is displayed, with the default widgets. Click on a widget to display more comprehensive information about the item (opens in the Edge browser)

Hot tip

Click on this **Menu** button for a specific widget, to access its menu for setting its size, and customizing it:

3 Scroll down the page to view the rest of the available widgets and their content

4 Move the cursor over a widget and click on this button in the top right-hand corner to close (hide) a widget

5 Click on the **Account** button in the top right-hand corner of the Widgets panel or the **Add widgets** button in Step 2 to access the Widgets settings panel. Click on categories to add them, or click on the **Personalize your interests** option

6 Options for managing items that appear in the Widgets panel are displayed. The left-hand panel contains categories of subjects that can be included. The right-hand panel contains a Search box and the most frequently used categories

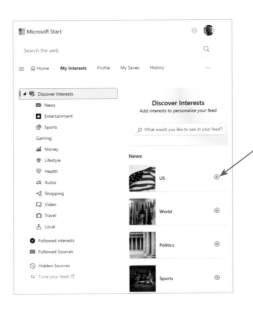

Don't forget

Click on the **+** icon in Step 6 to expand a category and view more options that can be included in the Widgets panel.

...cont'd

7 Click on one of the categories in the right-hand panel to select it and access more options for the category

8 Click on items within the selected category to view more levels for the subject. Select items as required

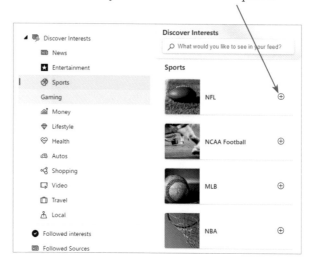

The **Followed interests** options are displayed in the Edge web browser.

9 Click on the **Followed interests** option in the left-hand panel to view subjects that you are following; these will appear in the Widgets panel

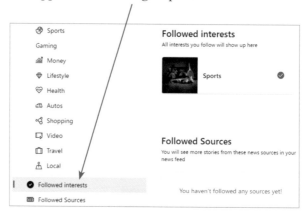

10 Enter a word or phrase into the **Discover Interests** Search box to find specific subjects. Click on one to find topics for the selected subject

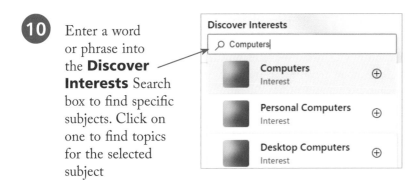

11 Click on the menu in Step 5 on page 35 and click on the **Privacy dashboard** option

Privacy dashboard

12 Select privacy options, as required, to determine how browsing, location and search data is used when accessing items, including those through the Widgets panel

Hot tip

Click on the **Clear your search history** button in Step 12 to view your search history from the Bing search engine and delete items, as required.

Hot tip

Click on a notification to open it and view its full contents.

Don't forget

Notifications for certain apps also appear on screen for a short period of time in a small banner, to alert you to the fact that there is a new notification.

Notifications

In the modern digital world there is an increasing desire to keep updated about what is happening in our online world. With Windows 11, the Notifications area can be used to display information from a variety of sources so that you never miss an update or a notification from one of your apps. To view your notifications:

1 Click here at the far right of the Taskbar. The number of new notifications is displayed

2 Notifications are displayed in the Notifications panel. Click on a notification to open it and view its full contents

3 Click on the **Clear all** button to remove all current notifications

Clear all

4 Click on the **Focus assist settings** option, at the top of the Notifications panel, to apply settings when notifications are not active; see pages 40-41

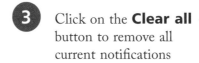

...cont'd

Settings for notifications

To change settings for notifications:

1 Click on the **Settings** app and click on the **System** tab

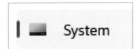

2 Click on the **Notifications** option

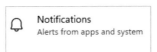

3 Drag the **Notifications** button **On**. Under the **Notifications from apps and senders** heading, drag the buttons **On** or **Off** to specify items that appear in the Notifications panel. For instance, if the **Mail** button is **On**, you will be notified whenever you receive a new email

Hot tip

Notifications can also be shown on the Lock screen by clicking on the down-pointing arrow next to the Notifications option and checking the **Show notifications on the lock screen** checkbox **On**.

4 Click on an app to specify how notifications operate for it. Options include showing banners on the screen when a notification arrives, and also for playing a sound – or not – for a notification

Notifications appear in their own panel on the screen and also in the Notifications panel. If Focus assist is used to restrict notifications from appearing, they will still be available in the Notifications panel.

Focus Assist

Notifications can be an excellent way to ensure that you never miss an important message or update. However, if there are too many notifications or they are appearing too frequently, it can become annoying if you are trying to concentrate on something else on your computer. To combat this, there are options for specifying how you receive notifications and how often. This is known as Focus assist, and it can be managed within the Settings app.

1 Open the Settings app and click on the **Focus assist** option within the **System** section

2 Check **On** the **Priority only** radio button to control which notifications appear on your computer. Click on the **Customize priority list** link

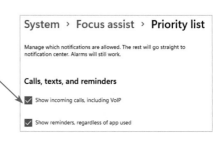

3 Check **On** or **Off** the options for notifications that come from a linked phone. This can be done for calls, texts and reminders

4 Check **On** the **Show notifications from pinned contacts on taskbar** checkbox to see these. Click on the **Add contacts** button to allow notifications from specific contacts

5 On the main Focus assist page, drag the buttons **On** or **Off** for specifying automatic rules for when notifications are displayed; e.g. during certain times or if you are playing a game

Click on each item in Step 5 to access options for specifying when notifications can be received, as in Step 6.

6 Click on the **During these times** option and specify times during which you do not want to receive any notifications

41

Settings

Accessing the Settings app

The Settings app in Windows 11 provide options for how you set up your computer and how it operates. There are 11 main Settings categories, each of which has a number of sub-categories.
To access and use the Settings app:

Some of the settings have been updated in Windows 11.

1   Click on the **Start** button

2   Click on the **Settings** button on the Start menu; or

3   Click on the **Settings** button on the Taskbar

Add the **Settings** app to the Taskbar for quick access. To do this, access it from the Start menu, right-click on it and click **Pin to Taskbar**.

In the **Settings** app, click on one of the main categories in the left-hand navigation panel to view the options within that category, in the main window.

If the Settings left-hand navigation panel is not visible (for instance, if the window has been reduced in size by resizing) click on this button on the top toolbar to view the navigation panel.

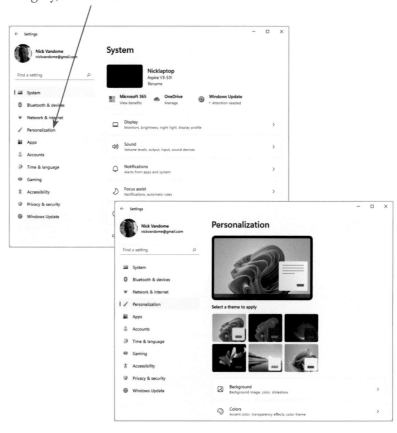

System settings

The System settings provide numerous options to specify how your computer looks and operates. They include:

- **Display**. This contains options for changing the size of items on the screen, the orientation of the screen, and options for adjusting the screen brightness, either manually or automatically.

The **Night light** feature in the **Display** setting can be used to apply a warmer color for the computer's display to create a more restful environment, particularly at night time.

- **Sound**. This contains options for selecting output and input devices for the sound on your PC, and for setting the volume.

- **Notifications**. This contains options for selecting which notification icons appear on the Taskbar and specifying which apps can be used to display notifications; e.g. your calendar and email apps.

Click on this button in the top left-hand corner of the Settings window to go back to the previously viewed page.

- **Focus assist**. This can be used to determine how notifications operate. See pages 40-41.

- **Power & battery**. This contains options for when the screen is turned off when not being used, and when the computer goes to sleep when it is not being used. This ranges from 1 minute to never.

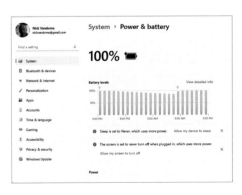

43

...cont'd

- **Storage**. This displays how much storage has been taken up on your computer and has options for where you want to save certain types of content. This can be the PC or an external drive, such as a hard drive or a USB flashdrive.

- **Nearby sharing**. This can be used to specify options for sharing files with other people, over a network.

- **Multitasking**. This contains options for working with windows and Desktops. Options can be set for snapping windows into position and for using multiple Desktops.

- **Activation**. This can be used to activate your copy of Windows 11, to confirm that it is an authorized version. Activation can be done online.

- **Troubleshoot**. This contains a range of options that can be used to identify, and in some cases fix, problems with software and hardware on your computer.

- **Recovery**. This can be used if you encounter problems with the way that Windows 11 is operating. You can select to refresh your computer and keep all of your files intact (although they should always be backed up first); reinstall Windows completely, which will reset it completely and you will lose all of your files and any apps you have downloaded; or return to an earlier version of Windows that was on your computer, without losing any files.

- **Projecting to this PC**. This can be used to allow other Windows 11 devices (computers, tablets or phones) to project their screens onto your computer so that you can view the screen and also interact with it.

- **Remote Desktop**. This contains options for controlling your PC from a remote device, with an appropriate app.

- **Clipboard**. This has options for saving multiple items to the clipboard and viewing them across different devices.

- **About**. This contains information about your computer and the version of Windows that you are using.

Don't forget

For more details about the Troubleshoot settings, see pages 218-219.

Bluetooth & devices settings

The Bluetooth & devices settings provide settings for how the hardware connected with your computer operates. They include:

- **Bluetooth**. This can be used to link your computer to compatible Bluetooth devices so that they can share content over short distances with radio waves. The two devices have to be "paired" initially to be able to share content.

- **Devices**. This can be used to connect to a Bluetooth device.

- **Printers & scanners**. This can be used to add new printers or scanners to your computer. These can either be wireless ones or ones that connect via cable. In most cases, the required software will be installed with Windows 11, or if not, it will be downloaded from the internet.

- **Your Phone**. This can be used to create a Bluetooth connection to your smartphone.

- **Cameras**. This can be used to connect a camera and download photos from it.

- **Mouse**. This contains options for customizing a connected mouse. These include setting the main button (**Left**, by default) and how scrolling operates with the mouse, such as the number of lines that can be scrolled at a time.

- **Touchpad**. This contains options for customizing a touchpad (for a laptop).

- **Pen & Windows Ink**. This contains options for using a stylus to jot down notes and sketch on the screen.

- **AutoPlay**. This contains options for applying AutoPlay for external devices such as removable drives and memory cards. If AutoPlay is **On**, the devices will be activated and accessed when they are attached to your computer.

- **USB**. This can be used to flag up any issues with connected USB devices.

Printers can also be added through the **Control Panel**. This is done in the **Devices and Printers** section, under **Hardware and Sound**. Click on the **Add a printer** button and follow the process.

The **Your Phone** setting can be used to link your PC and your smartphone so that tasks can be started on one device and then continued on another.

...cont'd

Network & internet settings

The Network & internet settings provide settings related to connecting to networks, usually for accessing the internet. They include:

If Wi-Fi is turned **On** in the Wi-Fi settings, any routers in range should be recognized. A password will probably then be required to connect to the router.

- **Wi-Fi**. This contains options for connecting to the internet via your Wi-Fi router (or public hotspots). There is also an option for managing your Wi-Fi networks.

- **Ethernet**. This can be used if you are connecting to the internet with an Ethernet cable. This connects to the Ethernet port on your computer, and internet access is delivered through the use of your telephone line.

- **VPN**. This can be used to connect to a corporate network over a VPN (Virtual Private Network). If you are doing this, you will need certain settings and details from your network administrator.

- **Mobile hotspot**. This can be used to determine how the computer interacts with mobile hotspots for connecting to shared public networks.

- **Airplane mode**. This can be used to turn off wireless communication when you are on a plane, so that you can still use your computer (laptop or tablet) safely.

- **Proxy**. This contains options for using a proxy server for Ethernet or Wi-Fi connections.

- **Dial-up**. This can be used if you have a dial-up modem for connecting to the internet. This is not common these days, but is still a valid means of internet access.

- **Advanced network settings**. This can be used to view details about, and change as required, the software and hardware settings for a network.

Personalization settings

The Personalization settings provide options for customizing the look and feel of Windows 11. They include:

- **Background**. This can be used to change the Desktop background in Windows 11. You can select images from the pictures provided, solid colors, a slideshow, or your own photos (using the **Browse photos** button). You can also choose how the background fits the screen (the default is **Fill**).

- **Colors**. This contains options for selecting a color for borders, buttons, the Taskbar and the Start menu background.

- **Themes**. This contains options for color themes that can be applied for several elements within the Windows 11 interface.

- **Lock screen**. This can be used to select a background for the Lock screen. You can use the images provided and also select your own photos (from the **Personalize your lock screen section**, change the drop-down option to **Picture** and then click the **Browse photos** button). You can also select apps that display relevant information on the Lock screen, such as email notifications or calendar events.

- **Touch keyboard**. This can be used to customize the appearance of the virtual on-screen keyboard, which can be used instead of a physical one.

- **Start**. This contains options for how the Start menu operates. It can be used to view the Start menu in full-screen mode and also display recently used items in the Start menu.

- **Taskbar**. This contains options for locking the Taskbar, automatically hiding it, changing the icon size, and specifying its screen location (**Left** or **Center**).

- **Fonts**. This displays the available fonts on your system and enables you to change their size.

- **Device usage**. This has a range of options for determining how you are contacted for items such as ads and recommendations from Microsoft.

In the Colors section there is an option for adding transparent effects.

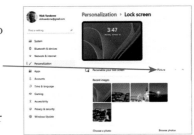

To access the touch keyboard, go to **Settings** > **Personalization > Taskbar** and drag the **Touch keyboard** button **On** under the **Taskbar corner icons** heading. This places the touch keyboard icon on the Taskbar; click on it to activate the keyboard.

...cont'd

Apps settings

The Apps settings provide options for specifying how apps work and interact with Windows 11. They include:

- **Apps & features**.
  This contains
  information about the
  apps that you have
  on your computer,
  including their size
  and installation

  date. There is also an option to specify how apps can be downloaded to your computer. Click on the **Choose where to get apps** drop-down box and select one of the options (**The Microsoft Store only (Recommended)** is the most secure option).

- **Default apps**. This can be
  used to select default apps
  for opening certain items
  such as email, music, photos
  and videos. Click on each
  app to select another default
  app, or look for one in the
  Microsoft Store.

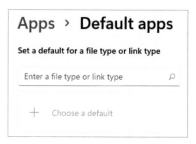

- **Offline maps**. This contains options for downloading maps so that you can use them even when you are offline. There is also an option for only downloading maps when you are connected to Wi-Fi, to save any unwanted charges if you have a mobile data plan.

- **Optional features**. This can be used to add features that can give additional functionality to apps within Windows 11.

- **Apps for websites**. This can be used to allow compatible apps to open websites, rather than using a browser.

- **Video playback**. This can be used to change the video settings for video playback apps.

- **Startup**. This can be used to specify apps that start when you log in to your Windows 11 account.

Accounts settings

The Accounts settings provide options for adding new online accounts (such as a new email account, or an online storage and sharing service such as Dropbox). They include:

- **Your info**. This displays information about your current account, which will either be the one you signed in to using your Microsoft Account details or a Local account, which has no online presence. You can also swap between accounts here.

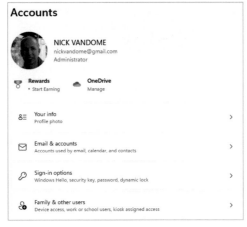

- **Email & accounts**. This can be used to add email accounts and also add a Microsoft Account.

- **Sign-in options**. This contains security options for signing in to your account. You can use facial or fingerprint recognition, with the correct reader devices, and create a PIN, Password or Picture password. Whichever method you choose, this will be required when you sign in to your account from the Lock screen.

- **Family & other users**. This can be used to set up accounts on your computer for other family members, or friends. They will be able to set their own sign-in options, and you will be able to switch users by clicking on the Start button and then clicking on the icon of the current user.

- **Windows backup**. This can be used to back up the files and apps on your computer to the OneDrive online backup and sharing service.

- **Access work or school**. This can be used to connect to a workplace network, where you can share certain items. To do this, you will need to contact the network administrator in order to obtain the correct settings to connect to the network.

The Accounts settings can be used to switch between a Microsoft Account and a Local account for signing in to your PC.

...cont'd

Time & language settings

The Time & language settings provide options for the time zone used by your computer, and the format for these items. They include:

- **Date & time**. This can be used to set the date and time, either manually or automatically, using the **Time zone** drop-down menu. There is also a link to **Related settings** in the Control Panel, where formatting options can be applied.

The date and time can be set manually by clicking on the **Change** button next to **Set the date and time manually** in the **Date & Time** section (**Set time automatically** must be turned **Off** first).

- **Language & region**. These two options can be used to select the language that is used by your computer; e.g. English (United States). You can also add new languages.

- **Typing**. This has options that can be applied for using the keyboard, including using Autocorrect and highlighting misspelled words.

- **Speech**. This contains options for how the speech function operates when using Windows 11. This includes the language to use when you are using speech, and also the default voice if using apps that speak text from the screen.

...cont'd

Gaming settings

The Gaming settings contain a range of options:

- **Xbox Game Bar**. This can be used for settings for the Game Bar controller that can be accessed when playing games with Windows 11.

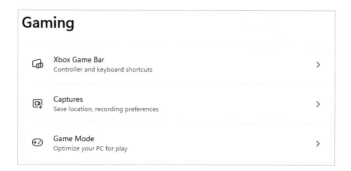

The Game Bar can be opened with keyboard shortcuts (**WinKey** + **G** by default), and it can be used to capture screenshots or video recordings of games being played. These can then be shared with other games.

- **Captures**. This contains options for capturing screenshots of games being played and game clips.

- **Game Mode**. This ensures the best possible gaming experience with Windows 11. Drag the **Game Mode** button **On** to activate it.

Don't forget

For more information about using the Xbox Console app and playing games with Windows 11, see pages 175-176.

...cont'd

Accessibility settings

The Accessibility settings are divided into three sections, for Vision, Hearing and Interaction. They include:

- **Text size**. This contains options for changing the size of text.

- **Visual effects**. This can be used to customize the show or hide scroll bars setting and apply transparency and animated effects.

- **Mouse pointer and touch**. This has options for changing the size and color of the on-screen mouse pointer.

- **Text cursor**. This has options for changing the size and color of the text cursor.

- **Magnifier**. This can be used to magnify what is being viewed on the screen, by up to 1600% of the standard view.

- **Color filters**. This can be used to apply color filters to the screen, to make photos and colors easier to see.

- **Contrast themes**. This contains options for applying high-contrast themes for Windows 11, to make certain elements more pronounced. This can be useful for users with dyslexia.

Don't forget

The Vision settings are: Text size, Visual effects, Mouse pointer and touch, Text cursor, Magnifier, Color filters, Contrast themes, and Narrator. The Hearing settings are: Audio and Captions. The Interaction settings are: Speech, Keyboard, Mouse, and Eye control.

- **Narrator**. This can be used to activate a screen reader so that text, buttons and toolbars can be read out loud.

- **Audio**. This can be used to change the device's volume, turn on mono audio, and display audio alerts visually.

- **Captions**. This can be used by hearing-impaired users to access and customize text subtitles for items such as movies or multimedia content.

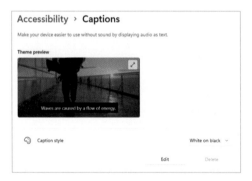

- **Speech**. This contains options for using voice dictation instead of using the keyboard for text entry.

- **Keyboard**. This can be used to enable the on-screen keyboard, and options for keyboard shortcuts and keyboard sounds for when certain keys are pressed.

- **Mouse**. This contains an option for using the numeric keypad for controlling the mouse pointer.

- **Eye control**. This is an option for using eye-control devices for entering content with a mouse and keyboard.

...cont'd

Privacy & security settings

The Privacy & security settings can be used for wide range of options for managing your data, and how it can be used by other people, and also security settings for keeping your computer as well protected as possible. They include:

- **Windows Security**. This contains settings for a wide range of security options, including virus protection and the Windows firewall. There is also a button for accessing the Window Security center.

You need to be signed in with your Microsoft Account in order for **Find my device** to work.

- **Find my device**. This contains settings for creating options for locating a lost Windows device.

- **For developers**. These are advanced settings, for people developing apps and services for Windows.

The Privacy & security Windows permissions section includes:

- **General**. This contains settings for general privacy options, including letting apps make advertising more specific to you, based on app usage, letting websites provide locally relevant content and letting Windows track app launches. There are also links to a range of information about privacy options, including a Privacy dashboard of items and a privacy statement.

- **Speech**. This can be used to train Windows and the personal digital assistant, Cortana, to your speaking style so that they can operate more efficiently.

- **Inking & typing personalization**. This can be used to create a personal dictionary based on your typing (and handwriting, if used) patterns.

- **Diagnostics & feedback**. This contains options for how feedback is sent to Microsoft.

- **Activity history**. This contains options for how Microsoft can collect information from the activities on your PC.

- **Search permissions**. This contains options for the type of content that is allowed to be viewed when searching on the web. The options are **Strict**, which filters out adult content; **Moderate**, which filters adult images and videos, but not text; and **Off**, which does not filter adult content. There are also options for searching the accounts on your computer.

The more access you give in terms of your own information and allowing apps to share your location, the more unwanted information you may be sent.

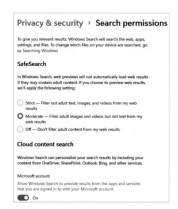

- **Searching Windows**. This can be used to specify which areas of your computer are searched. This can be either your Libraries and the Desktop or your entire computer. Specific folders can also be added, or excluded, from the locations to be searched.

The final part of the Privacy & security settings is **App permissions**. These can be used to apply settings for specific apps.

...cont'd

Windows Update settings

The Windows Update settings provide options for installing updates to Windows, and also backing up and recovering the data on your computer. They include:

Because of the nature of Windows 11 – e.g. it is designed as an online service – there will be regular updates. Check the **Windows Update** section regularly, even if you have set updates to be installed automatically, as you will be able to view the details of installed updates.

- **Windows Update**. This can be used to install system updates, such as those to Windows 11, and also important security updates. They can be set to be checked for and installed automatically (using the **Advanced options** section; see the next page) or manually (using the **Check for updates** button). For some updates, your computer will shut down and restart automatically. If updates are available, click on the **Download now** button.

Once updates have been downloaded, click on the **Install now** button.

- **Pause updates**. Use this to pause the update process for a week. If this is selected, a **Resume updates** button is available, if you want to start updates again within a week.

...cont'd

- **Update history**. This contains details about Windows updates that have been downloaded onto your computer.

- **Advanced options**. This contains options for receiving updates and managing restarts of your computer.

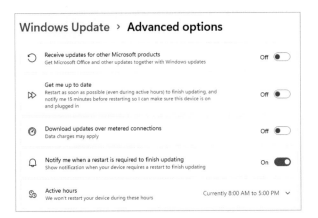

Click on the **Active hours** option in the **Advanced options** section to specify times during which your computer will not restart automatically, as a result of an update being installed.

- **Windows Insider Program**. This can be used to gain access to the Insider Program, for downloading preview versions of the latest Windows 11 updates.

Searching

Searching for items and information on computers and the internet has come a long way since the first search engines on the web. Most computer operating systems now have sophisticated search facilities for finding things on your own computer as well as searching over the web. They also now have personal digital assistants, which are voice-activated search functions that can be used instead of typing search requests.

Windows 11 has a Search box built in to the Taskbar. Separate searches can be performed with Cortana, the digital voice assistant (see pages 60-63).

Using the Search box for text searching

To use the Search box for text-only searches, over either your computer or the web:

Hot tip

The top search result is displayed at the top of the window in Step 3.

1 Click on this button on the Taskbar

2 The Search box is at the top of the window

3 Enter a search term (or website address)

4 Click on one of the results, or on one of the **See web results** buttons, to view the search results page in the Microsoft Edge browser

Hot tip

Click on the buttons at the top of the Search window to specify locations over which the search will be performed. These are **All**, **Apps**, **Documents**, **Web** and **More**.

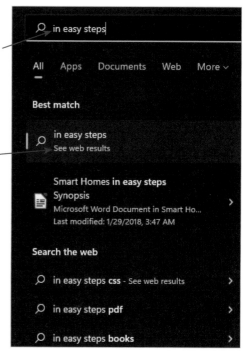

Asking a question

The Search box can also be used to ask specific questions.

1 Enter a question in the Search box

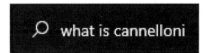

2 Click on the **See web results** button at the top of the Search box to view the results in the Microsoft Edge browser (in some instances, the answer will be displayed at the top of the Search box too)

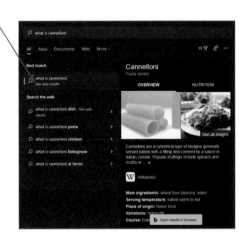

The magnifying glass icon indicates that a search is going to be undertaken on the web, and this will be displayed on a search results page, as in Step 2.

Searching over your computer

As well as searching over the web, the Search box can also be used to find items on your computer.

1 Enter a search query into the Search box and click on one of the options on the top toolbar to search for items from that location on your computer; e.g. Documents. Click on one of the results to open the item on your computer

If you are searching for a keyword over files on your computer, the search will be conducted over the text in documents and folders, not just the document titles. It will also search over the online backup and storage facility, OneDrive, if you have this set up (see pages 162-165).

59

Setting Up Cortana

To ensure that you can use Cortana to perform voice searches and queries, the language settings on your Windows 11 computer have to be set up correctly. To do this:

The county or region, display language and speech language should be the same in order for Cortana to work.

1 Open the **Settings** app and click on the **Time & language** tab

2 Click on the **Language & region** option

> Language & region
> Windows and some apps format dates and time based on your region

3 Click here to select a country or region

Region

Country or region
Windows and apps might use your country or region to give you local content — United States ∨

Regional format
Windows and some apps format dates and times based on your regional format — English (United States) ∨   ∨
ⓘ Some apps may need to be closed and reopened to see formatting changes.

4 Select a **Regional format**, which should match the region in Step 3

5 Click on the **Speech** option under **Time & language**

> Speech
> Speech language, speech recognition microphone setup, voices

6 Select the same **Speech language** as the one used as the display language in Step 4

Speech language

Choose the language you speak with your device

English (United States) ∨

Using Cortana

Voice searching with Cortana

As with text searches, Cortana can be used to search over various places and for different items.

1 Click on the Microphone button to the right of the Cortana box to begin a voice search

2 This symbol is displayed in the Search window to indicate that Cortana is listening

3 Cortana can be used for a wide range of general voice requests, which display the results from the web; e.g. ask about the capital city of a country and click on the result to see more details on the web

What is the capital of Madagascar?

Antananarivo, also known by its colonial shorthand form Tana, is the capital and largest city of Madagascar. The administrative area of the city, known as Antananarivo-Renivohitra, is the capital of Analamanga region. The city sits at 1,280 m above sea level in the center of the island, the highest national capital by elevation among the island countries. It has been the country's largest population center since at least the 18th century. The presidency, National Assembly, Senate and Supreme Court are located there, as are 21 diplomatic missions and the headquarters of many national and international businesses and NGOs. It has more universities, nightclubs, art venues, and medical services than any city on the island. Several national and local sports teams, including the championship-winning national rugby team, the Makis are based here.

Madagascar · Capital
Antananarivo

Bing   See more

Where's my next meeting?   What's the price of MSFT stock?   Create an appointment for Monday   Will it be sunny today?   Open Notepad

Ask Cortana

4 Queries can also be made in relation to the web; e.g. opening a specific website. Cortana can also be used to display specific information from the web, such as a weather forecast or sports results

Weather in New York.

Here's the current weather.

ALERT - Flash Flood - Watch

Rain showers   High 62°
61°F   Low 53°
New York
October 26, 11:03 AM

Bing   See more

Don't forget

Open the Cortana app from the Start menu to begin your voice search. The Cortana app can also be pinned to the Taskbar (see page 77).

Hot tip

Cortana can be used directly from the Lock screen to ask general queries such as "What is the weather in my area?" or to play a song from the Groove Music app.

...cont'd

5 If the query is general – e.g. "**Open Microsoft**" – various options in terms of apps from your computer will be displayed. Click on one of the apps to open it directly from Cortana

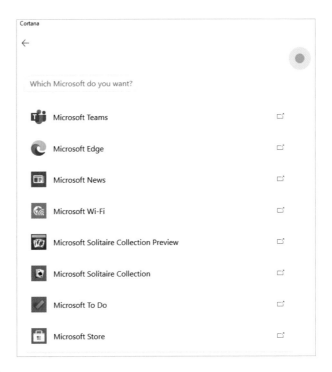

Cortana voice commands can be used to turn Off, Restart or put your PC to Sleep. They can also be used to change the system volume. Also, an increasing range of apps support Cortana, so can be used in conjunction with it; e.g. for playing movies with Netflix.

6 Cortana can be used to open specific apps; e.g. by saying "**Open Microsoft Edge**". If required, options will be available, depending on the request. Click on an item to access it

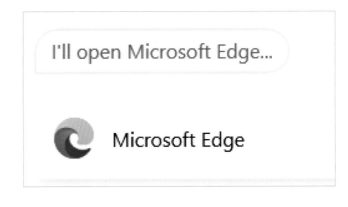

Cortana settings

A range of settings can be made for Cortana directly from the Cortana window when a search is being performed.

1 Open Cortana and click on the **Menu** button in the top left-hand corner of the Cortana window

2 Click on the **Settings** option

3 The Cortana settings are displayed

4 Click on the **Privacy** button in Step 3 to access options for specifying information Cortana can store about you, and how to clear data

5 Click on the **Microphone** button in Step 3 to access options to specify permissions for the microphone, and also for setting up **Voice activation**, for starting a Cortana search by saying "**Cortana**"

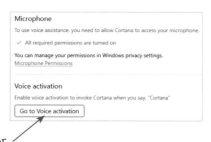

Adding and Switching Users

If more than one person uses the computer, each person can have a user account defined with a username and a password. To create a new user account, as either a Microsoft Account or a Local account:

1 Access the **Settings** app and click on the **Accounts** tab

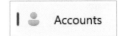

2 Click on the **Family & other users** option

- **Your info** — Profile photo
- **Email & accounts** — Accounts used by email, calendar, and contacts
- **Sign-in options** — Windows Hello, security key, password, dynamic lock
- **Family & other users** — Device access, work or school users, kiosk assigned access

3 In the **Add a family member** section, click the **Add account** button

Accounts › Family & other users

Your family

Let family members sign in to this PC—organizers can help keep members safer online with safety settings **Learn more about Family Safety**

Add a family member | Add account

4 Enter an email address for the new account and click on the **Next** button to access a window for adding a password. Then, click on the **Next** button again

Microsoft account

Add someone

Enter their email address

No Microsoft account? Create one for a child

Cancel | Next

5 Select a role for the new user, from **Organizer**, which offers more administration options, and **Member**

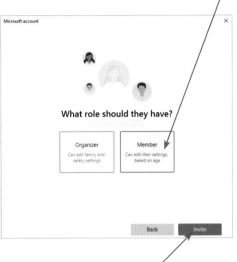

6 Click on the **Invite** button to complete the setup process

7 The user is added to the Accounts page

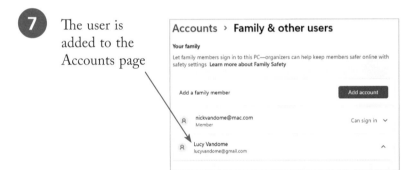

8 Click on a user to change the type of their account; e.g. from a Local account to a Microsoft Account, or to delete their account

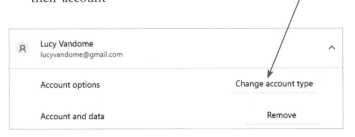

Don't forget

Multiple people can have separate accounts on the same computer, each with their own settings.

65

...cont'd

Switching users

If you have a number of user accounts defined on the computer (several accounts can be active at the same time), you do not need to close your apps and log off to be able to switch to another user. It is easy to switch back and forth.

1 Click on the **Start** button

2 Click on your own user account icon and click on another user's name. They will have to enter their own password in order to access their account, at which point they will be signed in. You can then switch between users without each having to log out every time

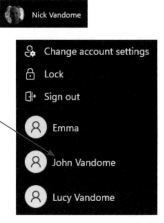

As an alternative way to switch users:

1 Press **WinKey** + **L** to lock the current user

2 Access the sign-in screen for all of the current users and select one as required

Shutting down

When you turn off your computer (see page 31), you will be warned if there are other user accounts still logged on to the computer.

1 Click on the **Shut down anyway** button to shut down without other users logging off

Someone else is still using this PC. If you shut down now, they could lose unsaved work.

Shut down anyway

Don't forget

When switching users, all of your settings and files are maintained but the new user will not be able to see them, and you will not be able to see theirs when you switch back. Your screen should look exactly the same as you left it.

66

Beware

If the other accounts have data files open, shutting down without logging them off could cause them to lose information.

3 Working with Apps

"Apps" is now a standard term in computing. Put simply, it is just another name for computer programs. In Windows 11, some apps are pre-installed, while thousands more can be downloaded from the Microsoft Store. This chapter shows how to work with and organize apps in Windows 11, and how to find your way around the Microsoft Store.

For Android users on smartphones and tablets, Android apps can also now be downloaded with Windows 11, which is a new feature.

In Windows 11, all apps open directly on the Desktop and their operation is more consistent, regardless of the type of app.

Starting with Apps

The word "app" is now firmly established as a generic term for computer programs on a range of devices. Originally, apps were items that were downloaded to smartphones and tablet computers. However, the terminology has now been expanded to cover any computer program. So, in Windows 11 most programs are referred to as "apps", although some legacy ones may still be referred to as "programs".

There are three main types of apps within Windows 11:

- **Windows 11 apps**. These are built-in apps that can be accessed from the Start menu. They cover the areas of communication, entertainment and information, and several of them are linked together through the online sharing service, OneDrive. In Windows 11, they open in their own window on the Desktop, in the same way as the older-style Windows apps (see below).

- **Windows classic apps**. These are older-style Windows apps that people may be familiar with from previous versions of Windows. These open in the Desktop environment.

- **Microsoft Store apps**. These are apps that can be downloaded from the online Microsoft Store and cover a wide range of subjects and functionality. Some Microsoft Store apps are free, while others have to be paid for.

Windows 11 apps

Windows 11 apps are accessed from the icons on the Start menu. Click on a tile to open the relevant app:

Windows classic apps

Windows classic apps are generally the ones that appeared as default with previous versions of Windows, and would have been accessed from the Start button. Windows classic apps can be accessed from the Start menu by using the alphabetic list, or searched for via the Taskbar Search box. Windows classic apps have the traditional Windows look and functionality, and they also open on the Desktop.

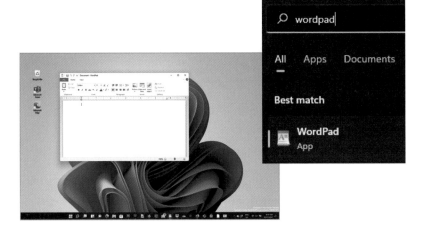

Microsoft Store apps

Microsoft Store apps are accessed and downloaded from the online Microsoft Store. Apps can be browsed and searched for in the Store, and when they are downloaded they are added to the **All apps** alphabetic list on the Start menu.

Don't forget

The Microsoft Store is accessed by clicking on the **Store** tile on the Start menu or on the Taskbar.

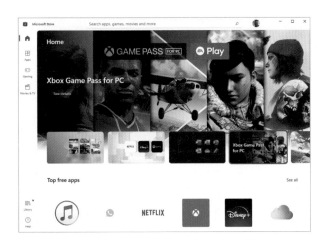

Windows 11 Apps

The Windows 11 apps that are accessed from the **All apps** alphabetic list on the Start menu cover a range of communication, entertainment and information functions. The apps include:

 Alarms & Clock. This provides alarms, clocks for times around the world, a timer and a stopwatch function.

 Calculator. This is a standard calculator that also has an option for using it as a scientific calculator.

 Calendar. This is a calendar that you can use to add appointments and important dates.

 Camera. This can be used to take photos directly onto your computer, but only if it has a built-in camera.

 Groove Music. This can be used to access the online Music Store where music can be downloaded.

 Mail. This is the online Mail facility. You can use it to connect to a selection of email accounts.

 Maps. This provides online access to maps from around the world. It also shows traffic issues.

 Microsoft Edge. This is the default browser in Windows 11 and is covered in detail in Chapter 9.

 Microsoft News. This is one of the information apps that provide real-time news information, based on your location.

 Microsoft Store. This provides access to the online Microsoft Store from where a range of other apps can be bought and downloaded to your computer.

Microsoft Teams. This is Microsoft's collaboration and communication app that can be used for personal or business use. Windows 11 also includes the Chat app, available from the Taskbar only, which is a pop-out version of the Teams audio-, video- and text-chatting functions.

 Microsoft To Do. This is Microsoft's own list-making app that can also be used to set reminders. If you are logged in with your Microsoft Account, the app can also be used with Mail, Outlook and Cortana.

Some of these apps may not be supplied as standard on your Windows 11 system, but you can get them from the Microsoft Store (see pages 79-81).

If you have updated to Windows 11 from a version of Windows 10, some of the apps and their icons may be imported from Windows 10 and may appear slightly different than in Windows 11 installed on a new computer.

See Chapter 10 for more information about working with the Calendar, Mail, People and Chat apps, and how content can be shared between different apps.

The Microsoft To Do app is a new feature in Windows 11.

70

Movies & TV (**Films & TV** in some regions). This is where you will see the movies and TV shows you buy in the Microsoft Store. There is also a link to the Video Store.

 OneDrive. This is an online facility for storing and sharing content from your computer. This includes photos and documents.

 OneNote. This is a Microsoft note-taking app, part of the Office suite of apps.

 Outlook. Part of Microsoft's 365 subscription service, containing mail, calendar, contacts and tasks options.

 Paint 3D. This is an app that can be used to create, view and share 3D objects.

 Photos. This can be used to view and organize your photos. It can also be used to share and print photos.

 Settings. This can be used to access all of the main settings for customizing and managing Windows 11 and your computer. (See pages 42-57 for details.)

 Snipping Tool. This can be used to capture and annotate screenshots: an image of the screen being viewed.

 Sticky Notes. This is an app for creating short notes that can be "stuck" to the screen so that they are readily visible.

 Voice Recorder. This can be used to record, save and share audio messages.

 Weather. This provides real-time weather forecasts for locations around the world.

 Xbox. This can be used to download and play games, and also play online Xbox games.

A Desktop app for OneDrive can also be downloaded from the Microsoft Store. This can be used to view and manage folders and files in OneDrive. The version described on the pages here is the File Explorer version of OneDrive, where the folders and files are displayed in File Explorer.
App versions of OneDrive can also be downloaded for iOS and Android devices.
OneDrive can also be used to share your content, such as photos and documents, with other people. See pages 162-165 for details.

By default, the Weather app will provide the nearest forecast to your location, if you have given permission for this in **Settings** > **Privacy & security** > **Location**.

71

Using Windows 11 Apps

In Windows 11, all of the apps have been designed to have as consistent an appearance as possible. However, due the age of some apps, there are still some differences.

Windows 11 apps

Windows 11 apps open in their own window on the Desktop and they can be moved and resized in the same way as older-style Windows apps.

1   Click and drag on the top toolbar to move the app's window and reposition it

In Windows 11 there has been a conscious effort to achieve a greater consistency between the newer-style apps and the old, classic-style apps.

2   Drag on the bottom or right-hand border to resize the app's window (or the bottom right-hand corner to resize the height and width simultaneously)

...cont'd

Windows 11 app menus
Some Windows 11 apps have their own menus.

1 Click on this button (if available) within the app's window to access its menu

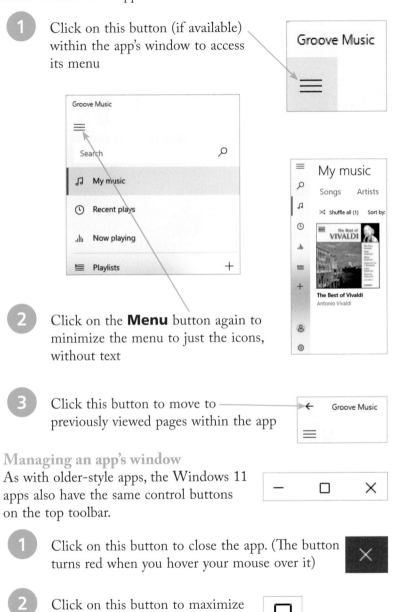

2 Click on the **Menu** button again to minimize the menu to just the icons, without text

Don't forget

Apps that are installed from a CD or DVD are automatically included on the alphabetical list on the Start menu.

3 Click this button to move to previously viewed pages within the app

← Groove Music
≡

Managing an app's window
As with older-style apps, the Windows 11 apps also have the same control buttons on the top toolbar.

— ☐ ✕

1 Click on this button to close the app. (The button turns red when you hover your mouse over it)

✕

2 Click on this button to maximize the app's window

☐

3 Click on this button to minimize the app's window (it will be minimized onto the Taskbar)

—

Classic Apps on the Desktop

The Windows classic apps open on the Desktop, in the same way as with previous versions of Windows, even though they are opened from the Start menu (or the Taskbar).

Opening a Windows classic app

To open a Windows classic app:

1 Click on the **Start** button and navigate through the app list

2 Select the app you want to open (for example, WordPad from the **Windows Tools** section)

3 The app opens on the Desktop

Hot tip

If apps have been pinned to the Taskbar, as shown on page 77, they can be opened directly from there by simply clicking on them.

4 Click on the tabs at the top of the app to access relevant Ribbon toolbars and menus

Closing Apps

There are several ways to close a Windows app.

1 Click on the red **Close** button at the top right of the window

2 Select **File** > **Exit** from the File menu (if available)

3 Press **Alt** + **F4**

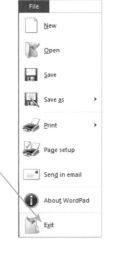

The **Close** button only turns red when you hover your mouse over it.

It is always worth saving a new document as soon as it is created. It should also be saved at regular intervals as you are working on it.

4 Right-click on the icon on the Taskbar and select **Close window** (or **Close all windows** if more than one is open)

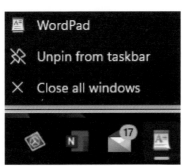

5 If any changes have been made to the document, you may receive a warning message advising you to save the associated file

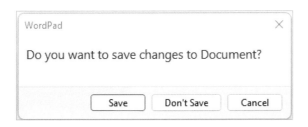

Searching for Apps

As you acquire more and more apps, it may become harder to find the ones you want. To help with this, you can use the Search box to search over all of the apps on your computer. To do this:

1 Click in the Search box on the Taskbar

2 Enter a word in the Search box

3 As you type, relevant apps are displayed. When the one you are seeking appears, click on it to open the app

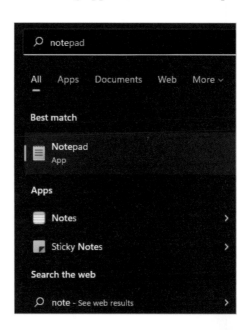

You just have to put in the first couple of letters of an app and Search will automatically suggest results based on this. The more that you type, the more specific the results become. Case does not matter when you are typing a search.

4 Click on the **Apps** tab to view results relating only to apps

5 The Apps tab also displays an option for searching for related apps in the Microsoft Store

Pin to Taskbar

All apps can be pinned to the Desktop Taskbar (the bar that appears along the bottom of the Desktop) so that they can be accessed quickly. To do this:

1 Click on the **Start** button to access the Start menu and a full list of apps

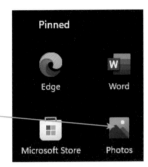

2 Right-click on an app and click on **Pin to taskbar**

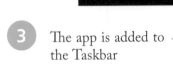

Apps can be unpinned from the Taskbar by right-clicking on them and selecting **Unpin from taskbar** from the contextual menu that appears.

3 The app is added to the Taskbar

4 Open apps on the Taskbar can also be pinned there by right-clicking on them and selecting **Pin to taskbar**

5 Pinned items remain on the Taskbar even once they have been closed

Pin to Start Menu

In most cases, you will want to have quick access to a variety of apps on the Start menu, not just the Windows 11 apps. It is possible to "pin" any app to the Start menu so that it is always readily available. To do this:

1 Access the alphabetical list of apps, from the Start button

Hot tip

Apps can be unpinned from the Start menu by right-clicking on them and selecting **Unpin from Start** from the menu that appears.

2 Right-click on an app and click on the **Pin to Start** button

3 The app is pinned to the Start menu

Using the Microsoft Store

The third category of apps that can be used with Windows 11 are
those that are downloaded from the Microsoft Store. These cover
a wide range of topics, and they provide an excellent way to add
functionality to Windows 11. To use the Microsoft Store:

1 Click on the **Microsoft Store** tile
on the Start menu, or the Taskbar

2 The currently featured apps are displayed on
the Home screen

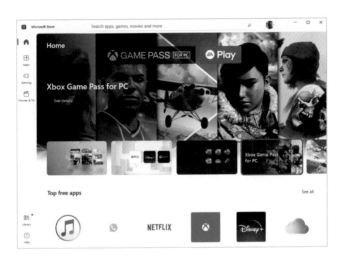

Windows 11 apps can
be downloaded from the
Microsoft Store.

3 Scroll up and down to see additional items and categories

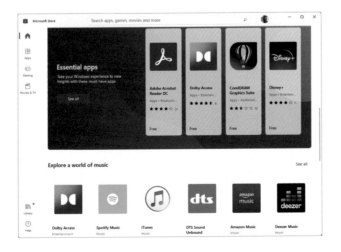

...cont'd

4 Scroll down the Homepage, then click on the **See all** button next to a category; e.g. **Top free apps**

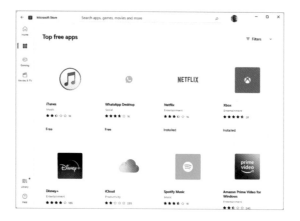

Don't forget

Scroll up and down in Step 6 to view ratings and reviews about the app, and also any additional descriptions.

5 The full range of apps for the selected category are displayed. Swipe up and down the page to view them

6 Click on an app to preview it, and for more details

7 On the **See all** page, click on the **Filters** button

8 Click the options for how the apps selection is filtered; e.g. **Top free**

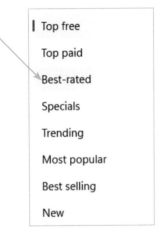

9 Click on a new category for filtering the app selection; e.g. **Best-rated**

Top free

Top paid

Best-rated

Specials

Trending

Most popular

Best selling

New

10 Enter a word or phrase into the **Search apps, games, movies and more** box on the top toolbar to see matching apps. Click on a result to view the related app

Search apps, games, movies and more

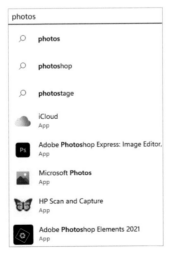

Don't forget

As more characters are added to the Search box in Step 10, the search results will become more defined; i.e. a closer match to what appears in the Search box.

Buying Apps

When you find an app that you want to use, you can download it to your computer. To do this:

1 Click on the app and click on the **Get** (or price) button

Cut Paste Photos
Z Mobile Apps

Get

+ Offers in-app purchases

If there is a fee for an app, this will be displayed instead of the **Get** button. You will need to have credit/debit card details registered on your Microsoft Account in order to buy paid-for apps (**Settings > Accounts > Your info > Accounts > Manage my accounts**).

2 The app downloads from the Microsoft Store and a **Downloading** message is displayed

Downloading: 11.04 MB of 103.4 MB ..

3 The app is added to the Start menu and has a **New** tag next to it. This disappears once the app has been opened

Cut Paste Photos
New

4 Click on the app to open and use it (initially it will be available under the **Recommended** section of the Start menu, as **Recently added**, as well as having its own alpha listing)

Recommended

Cut Paste Photos
Recently added

Viewing Your Apps

As you download more and more apps from the Microsoft Store, you may lose track of which ones you have obtained and when. To help with this, you can review all of the apps you have downloaded, from within the Microsoft Store. To do this:

1 Open the Microsoft Store and click on the **Library** button

Library

2 All of the apps that have been downloaded are displayed

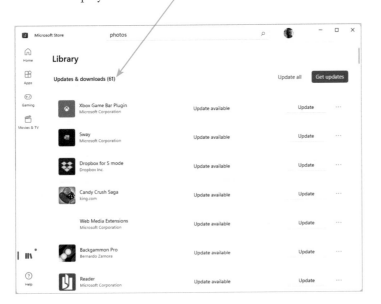

Don't forget

You can reinstall apps from the **Downloads** section, even if you have previously uninstalled them. If there was a fee for an app, you will not have to pay again to reinstall it.

83

3 Tap on the **Get updates** button to see if there are any updates for the listed apps

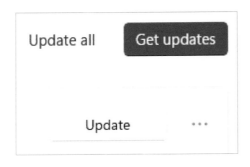

Hot tip

To set apps to be updated automatically, open the Microsoft Store and click on your account icon at the top of the screen. Click on the **App settings** button and drag the **App updates** button **On**.

Android Apps

Android apps are widely used on Android smartphones, and it is now possible to download some of the same apps with Windows 11 so that Android users can synchronize some features between their smartphones and desktop or laptop computers. Android apps can be accessed from the Amazon Appstore, via the Microsoft Store. To use Android apps with Windows 11:

Being able to access Android apps is a new feature in Windows 11.

1 Open the Microsoft Store app, from either the Taskbar or the Start menu

2 Enter "**android**" into the Microsoft Store Search box. The Android app options are displayed

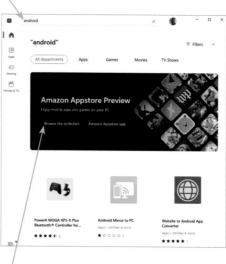

The Android apps feature did not have its full functionality with the initial Windows 11 release, although this will be enhanced with subsequent updates.

3 Click on the **Browse the collection** button in Step 2 to download the Amazon Appstore app, from where Android apps can be downloaded

Default Apps

Certain apps can be assigned for specific file types, so if you open that file type – i.e. by double-clicking on it in File Explorer – it will open in the default app. This can be applied for numerous file types, from within the Settings app. To do this:

1 Open the **Settings** app and click on the **Apps** option

2 Click on the **Default apps** option

3 Click on an app to use it as the default for specific file types

Photos

4 The file types that are opened by default by the app are displayed. Click on one to change the default app

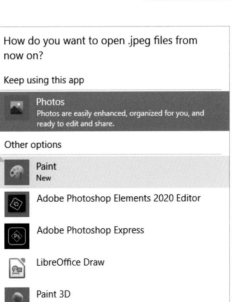

5 Click on another app, as required, for the file type, to set the app as the default for opening this file type. Click on the **OK** button

The original default apps for opening file types are most Windows ones. However, this can also be changed to non-Windows ones for most file types.

Install and Uninstall

Installing apps from a CD or DVD

If the app you want to install is provided on a CD or DVD, you normally just insert the disc. The installation app starts up automatically, and you can follow the instructions to select features and complete the installation. If this does not happen automatically:

1 Insert the disc. If it does not run automatically, right-click on the Start button and click on the **Run** option

2 Navigate to the disc in the File Explorer sidebar and click on the **autorun.exe** file

Installation files can also be named **Set-up.exe** when accessed in Step 2.

3 Click on the **Open** button

4 The file is added to the **Run** window

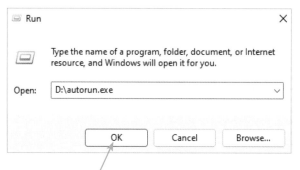

5 Click on the **OK** button to run the file and install the program, which can then be accessed from the Start menu

Uninstalling apps

In some previous versions of Windows, apps were uninstalled through the Control Panel. However, in Windows 11, pre-installed Microsoft apps (and Microsoft ones that have been downloaded from the Microsoft Store) can be uninstalled directly from the Start menu. To do this:

1 Right-click on an app to access its menu

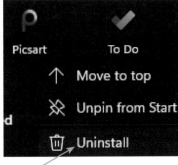

A greater range of apps can be uninstalled in Windows 11. If the **Uninstall** option is not available in Step 1, the app cannot be uninstalled; e.g. the Microsoft Edge app.

2 Click on the **Uninstall** button

3 A window alerts you to the fact that related information will be removed if the app is uninstalled. Click on the **Uninstall** button if you want to continue

To get to the Control Panel, right-click on the Start button and select **Control Panel** from the Power User menu.

4 If an app has been uninstalled, it will no longer be available from the list of apps on the Start menu. However, it can be downloaded again from the Microsoft Store

If apps have been installed from a CD or DVD, they can also still be uninstalled from within the Control Panel. To do this, select the **Programs** section and click on the **Uninstall a Program** link. The installed apps will be displayed. Select one of the apps and click on the **Uninstall/Change** link.

Some elements of Windows 11, such as the Control Panel, still refer to apps as programs, but they are the same thing.

Task Manager

Task Manager lists all the apps and processes running on your computer; you can monitor performance or close an app that is no longer responding.

To open Task Manager:

1 Right-click on the **Start** button and select **Task Manager**, or press **Ctrl** + **Shift** + **Esc** on the keyboard

2 When Task Manager opens, details of the currently running apps are displayed

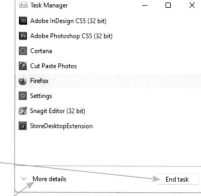

3 If an app is given the status of **Not Responding** and you cannot wait for Windows to fix things, select the app and click on the **End task** button

4 Click on the **More details** button to view detailed information about the running apps. Click on the **Processes** tab to show the system and the current user processes. The total CPU usage and the amount being used by each process are shown as (continually varying) percentages

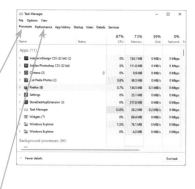

5 Click on the **Performance** tab to see graphs of recent CPU and memory usage and other details

4 Standard Controls

Even in Windows 11, much of what you do will be with menus, dialog boxes and windows, as used in many versions of Windows. This chapter shows how to use these elements and how you can control and manage working with folders and files in Windows 11.

Menus

Traditionally, windows have a tabbed Menu bar near the top, displaying the menu options relevant to that particular window. Some Menu bars consist of drop-down menus, and others are in the format of the Ribbon, also known as the Scenic Ribbon.

Drop-down menus

For apps such as WordPad, the Menu bar consists of tabbed drop-down menus.

 Open an app and click or tap on one of the Menu bar options to view its details

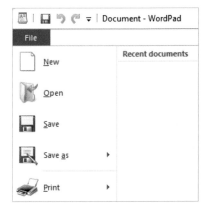

Scenic Ribbon

For apps such as WordPad (and Office apps) there is a Ribbon (or Scenic Ribbon) at the top of the window with the Menu bar tabs.

 Open an app and select one of the Menu bar tabs on the Ribbon to view its details

Some options may have shortcut keys associated with them (e.g. **Alt** + **Up arrow** – Up one level), so you can use these instead of using your mouse. Other examples of shortcut keys are:

Ctrl + **A** – Select All   **Ctrl** + **C** – Copy   **Ctrl** + **V** – Paste
Ctrl + **X** – Cut   **Ctrl** + **Y** – Redo   **Ctrl** + **Z** – Undo

---

The Menu bar is not always displayed in folder windows. Press the **Alt** key to display it temporarily.

The WordPad app can be accessed from the **Windows Tools** option on the Start menu or by using the Search box at the top of the Start menu.

An ellipsis (**...**) indicates that if this option is selected, an associated window with further selections will be displayed.

If an option is grayed out (dimmed out), it is not available for use at this particular time or is not appropriate.

Dialog Boxes

Although simple actions can be made quickly from menu options, more specific settings are made from windows displayed specifically for this purpose. These are called dialog boxes.

Tabs
Some dialog boxes are divided into two or more tabs (grouped options). Only one tab can be viewed at a time.

Checkboxes
Select as many as required. A check mark indicates that the option is active. If you select it again it will be turned off. If an option is grayed out, it is unavailable and you cannot select it.

Radio buttons
Only one out of a group of radio buttons can be selected. If you select another radio button, the previously selected one is automatically turned off.

Command buttons
OK will save the settings selected and close the dialog box or window. **Cancel** will close the dialog box or window, discarding any amended settings. **Apply** will save the settings selected so far but will not close the dialog box or window, enabling you to make further changes.

Beware

Dialog boxes are usually fixed-size windows and therefore do not have scroll bars, minimize and maximize buttons or resize pointers.

Hot tip

These examples are from the Folder Options dialog box. To access it, click on the **Menu** button on the File Explorer Menu bar, and click on **Options**.

Structure of a Window

You can have a window containing icons for further selection, or a window that displays a screen from an app. All these windows are similar in their structure. This example is from File Explorer (see page 122).

Forward and Back   Address bar   Menu bar

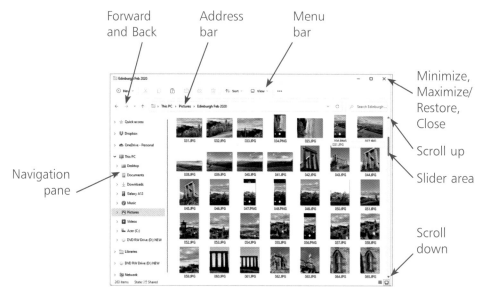

Minimize, Maximize/ Restore, Close

Scroll up

Slider area

Navigation pane

Scroll down

File Explorer has been updated in Windows 11, to include a new Menu bar at the top of the File Explorer window, rather than the Scenic Ribbon that previously used to navigate around File Explorer, as with some apps. This is a new feature in Windows 11.

Scroll bars will only appear when there are items that cannot fit into the current size of the window.

If you move the mouse pointer over any edge of a window, the pointer changes shape and becomes a double-headed Resize arrow – drag it to change the size of a window (see page 95).

Double-click on an icon to open a window relating to it – in this case, a WordPad application window. This window has a Menu bar, Ribbon, ruler, and a Control icon at the top left.

Moving a Window

As long as a window is not maximized – i.e. occupying the whole screen – you can move it. This is especially useful if you have several windows open and need to organize your Desktop.

1 Move the mouse pointer over the Title bar of a window

You will see the whole window move, with the full contents displayed and transparency still active while you are dragging the window.

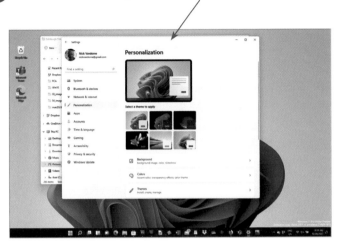

If you have two monitors attached to your system, you can extend your Desktop onto the second monitor and drag a window from one monitor onto the other.

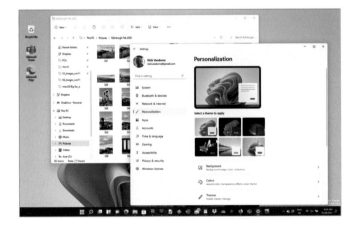

2 Drag the mouse pointer across the Desktop (left-click and hold, or tap and hold as you move)

3 When the window reaches the desired location, release to relocate the window there

Restoring a Window

Within the Desktop environment there are a number of actions that can be performed on the windows within it. A window can be maximized to fill the whole screen, minimized to a button on the Taskbar or restored to the original size.

You can also double-click or tap the **Title bar** to maximize a window. Repeat the process to restore it to the original.

You can also use Snap Assist to maximize, move or resize windows (see pages 96-97).

Original-size window   Maximize button   Maximized window

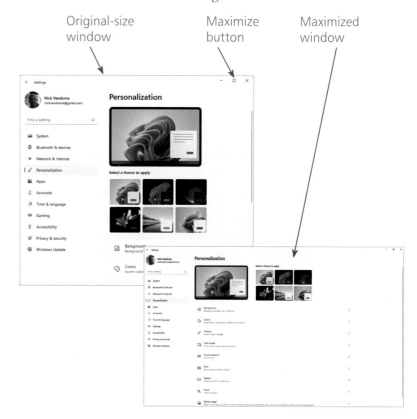

You can right-click the Title bar area to display the Control context menu.

Whether a window is maximized or original-size, click on the **Minimize** button (left of the top-right three buttons) to reduce the window to its Taskbar icon. This will create space on the Desktop for you to work in other windows. When you want to restore the reduced window, simply select its **Taskbar** icon.

The middle button is the **Maximize** button. Or, if the window is already maximized, the button changes to the **Restore** button.

Click **Close**, the third button, when you want to close an app or to close a window.

Resizing a Window

If a window is not maximized or minimized, it can be resized.

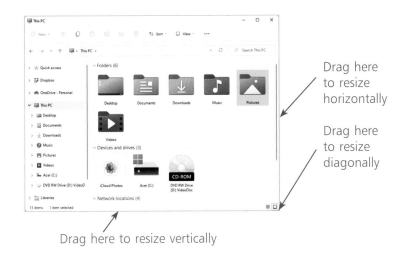

Drag here to resize horizontally

Drag here to resize diagonally

Drag here to resize vertically

Resize and move all of the windows on your Desktop to organize the layout to the way you prefer to work, or see pages 96-99 for other ways of arranging windows.

1 Place the mouse arrow anywhere on the edge of a window or on any of the corners. The pointer will change to a double-headed Resize arrow

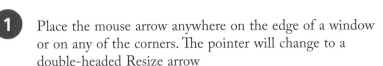

Click, or tap, and drag the arrow outward to increase the size of the window, or inward to reduce the size.

Resizing a window using keyboard shortcuts
Alternatively, you may want to use the keyboard keys to resize a window.

The **Size** command is not available if the window is maximized.

1 Press **Alt** + **Space bar**

2 Press **S** and the mouse pointer will change to a four-headed arrow

3 Use the Left, Right, Up or Down arrow keys on your keyboard to adjust the size of the window

4 Press **Enter** when the window is resized as required

95

Snap Assist

Snap Assist provides a set of methods for resizing and moving windows around the Desktop.

Maximize fully

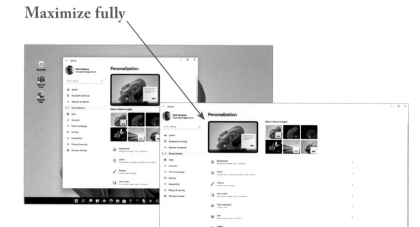

If the window you want to maximize is not the current one, click on it first before carrying out the maximize operation.

Click and hold the Title bar and drag the window up the screen. As the mouse pointer reaches the top edge of the screen, the window maximizes. The shortcut is **WinKey** + **Up arrow**.

Maximize vertically

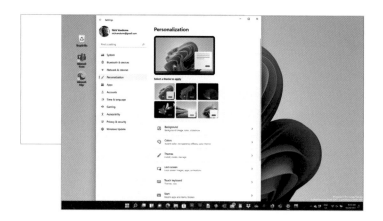

Click or tap and hold the top border of the window (until it turns into a double-headed arrow), and drag it toward the top edge of the screen. When the mouse pointer reaches the edge of the screen, the window will maximize in the vertical direction only. The shortcut is **WinKey** + **Shift** + **Up arrow**.

...cont'd

Snap to the left

When you click the Title bar on an app such as WordPad, be sure to avoid the tools on the Quick access toolbar.

To position the window to fill the left-hand side of the screen, click (or tap) the Title bar and drag it to the left. As the mouse pointer reaches the left edge, the window resizes to fill half of the screen. The shortcut is **WinKey + Left arrow**. If other apps are open they will be shown as thumbnails in the right-hand panel.

Snap to the right
To position the window to fill the right-hand side of the screen, click or tap the Title bar and drag it to the right. As the mouse pointer reaches the right edge, the window resizes to fill half of the screen. The shortcut key is **WinKey + Right arrow**.

Compare two windows
Snap one of the windows to the left and the other window to the right.

Restore
Drag the Title bar of a maximized or snapped window away from the edge of the screen and the window will return to its previous size (though not the same position). The shortcut is **WinKey + Down arrow**.

Windows can also be shown side-by-side, and also other formats, using the **Snap Layouts** feature; see pages 98-99.

Double-clicking or tapping the Title bar will also reverse the maximize or snap. This restores size and position.

97

Snap Layouts

Windows 11 provides great flexibility when it comes to working with windows: it is possible to display up to four active windows at a time, in a range of formats. This is known at Snap Layouts, which can be accessed from the control buttons at the top of any window. To use Snap Layouts:

The Snap Layouts function has been updated in Windows 11.

1 Open an app and move the cursor over this button in the right-hand corner of the window. This displays the Snap Layouts panel

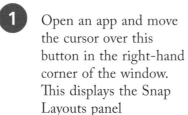

Beware

Don't click on the button in Step 1 as this will maximize the window.

2 Click on one of the thumbnails in the Snap Layouts panel

Beware

Not all third-party apps support the Snap Layouts feature.

3 The app is displayed in the position selected in Step 2

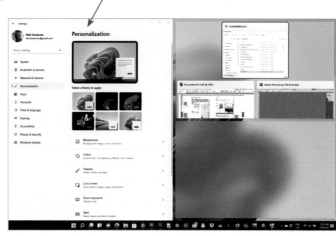

98

4 If there are other open apps, they will be displayed as thumbnails in one of the available Snap Layouts panel. Click on one of the thumbnails to maximize the selected app in the panel

Don't forget

Apps can be rearranged once they have been assigned a position in a Snap Layout, by accessing the Snap Layout as in Step 1 on the previous page, and selecting a new location for the app.

5 Open another app and repeat the process in Steps 1 and 2 to position it as required

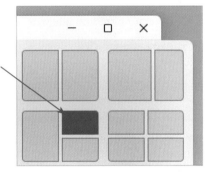

Don't forget

Apps can be "unsnapped" from their positions, by clicking and holding on the Title bar and dragging them into a new position.

6 The app is displayed in the position selected in Step 5

Switching Windows

If you have several windows open on your Desktop, only one will be active. This will be the foremost window and it has its Title bar, Menu bar and outside window frame highlighted. If you have more than one window displayed on the Desktop, select anywhere inside a window that is not active to activate it and switch to it.

Active window   Active task button

Another method of switching windows is to use the Taskbar at the bottom. Every window that is open has an icon button created automatically on the Taskbar. Therefore, it does not matter if the window you want to switch to is overlaid with others and you cannot see it. Just select the button for it in the Taskbar, and the window will be moved to the front and made active.

Move the mouse pointer over a task button, and a Live Preview is displayed (one for each window if there are multiple tasks).

Don't forget

You can click on the preview to select that item and bring its window to the front of the Desktop.

Arranging Icons

You can rearrange the order of the items in your File Explorer folders, or on your Desktop, in many different ways.

1 Right-click in a clear area (of the File Explorer folder or the Desktop) to display a shortcut context menu

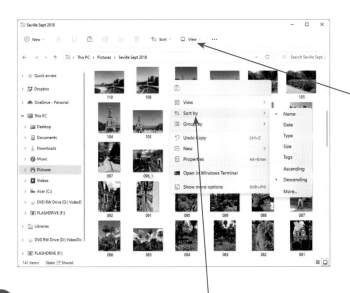

Select the **View** button in Step 1 to cycle through a range of views for File Explorer.

2 Move the pointer over **Sort by** to reveal a submenu of sorting options and click or tap the **Name** option – for example – to sort all the file icons in ascending name order

3 Select **Name** a second time and the files will be sorted in descending name order

Group by

You can select **Group by** for folder windows (but not for the Desktop). This groups your files and folders alphabetically by name, size, type, etc.

Closing a Window

When you have finished with a window you will need to close it. There are several ways of doing this – use the method that is easiest and the most appropriate at the time.

Open window

If the top-right corner of the window is visible on the Desktop:

1 Select the **Close** button on the Title bar

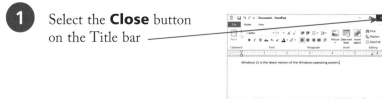

Minimized window

For a window that is minimized or one that is hidden behind other windows:

1 Move the mouse pointer over the associated Taskbar icon button

2 Click on the **Close** button

Control menu

If only part of the window is visible on the Desktop:

1 Select the **Control** icon (top-left corner) or right-click the Title bar

2 Select **Close** on the Control menu

Keyboard

To close any type of window, use this key combination:

1 Select the window to make it the current active window, then press **Alt** + **F4** to close the window

5 Customizing Windows

The Desktop environment is still an important one in Windows 11, and this chapter looks at how to work with it and personalize the elements of Windows 11 to your own requirements and preferences, with colors, themes and sounds.

Personalization

Customizing the look and feel of Windows 11 is a good way to make it feel like it is your own personal device. This can be done with some of the options in the Personalization section of the Settings app. This includes customizing the Desktop background.

Click in the **Personalize your background** section in Step 2 and select an option for the background, from **Picture**, **Solid color** or **Slideshow**.

| Picture

Solid color

Slideshow

1 Open the **Settings** app and click on the **Personalization** tab

2 Click on the **Background** option to select a new Desktop background

3 The image selected in Step 2 becomes the Desktop background

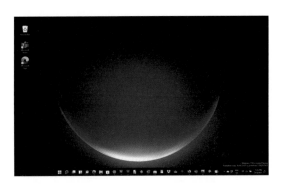

4 To select one of your own pictures for the Desktop background, click on the **Browse photos** button next to the **Choose a photo** option

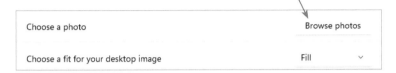

5 Browse to the required photo, select it, and click on the **Choose picture** button

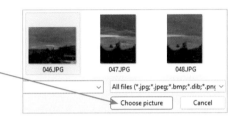

6 The photo is added to the **Background** section of the Personalization settings, and remains available here even if another background is selected

Click in the **Choose a fit for your desktop image** box to specify how the picture fills the background screen. The options are: **Fill**, **Fit**, **Stretch**, **Tile**, **Center**, and **Span**.

7 The photo is added as the Desktop background

...cont'd

Personalizing colors

Many of the color elements of Windows 11 can also be personalized. To do this:

1 Within the Personalization settings, click on the **Colors** option

2 The color personalization options are displayed within the main Colors window

The **Light** and **Dark** options in Step 4 are applied to the Taskbar and the Start menu.

3 For the **Choose your mode** option, click here

4 Select an option for the colors for the Windows 11 interface, from **Light**, **Dark**, or **Custom**

Light

Dark

| Custom

5 The same color options as in Step 4 can also be selected for the **Choose your default Windows mode** and **Choose your default app mode** options

Choose your default Windows mode

Choose your default app mode

6 Drag the **Transparency effects** button **On** to enable the background behind a window to show through it to a certain degree

7 Turn the **Show accent color on Start and taskbar** and **Show accent color on title bars and windows borders** options **On** or **Off**, as required

8 To select your own colors for accent colors, click on the **Accent color** section and select the **Manual** option

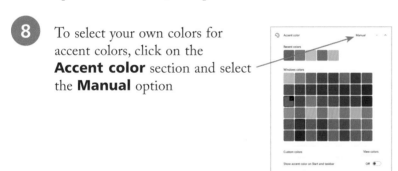

9 Click on the **View colors** button

10 Click on an area of the color chart to select a new color and click on the **Done** button

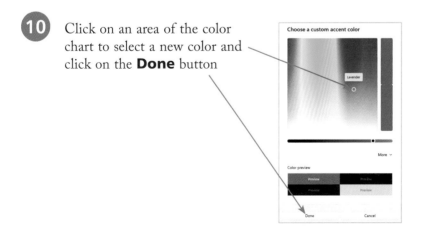

Hot tip

If the **Transparency effects** button is **On**, the colors behind a window will change as the window is moved around the screen.

107

Using Themes

Themes in Windows 11 can be used to customize several items for the look and feel of Windows.

1 Open **Settings** and click on the **Personalization** tab

2 Click on the **Themes** option

3 The current theme is displayed

4 Make a selection for a customized theme, using **Background**, **Color**, **Sounds** and **Mouse cursor**

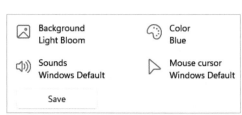

Don't forget

The preset themes in Step 5 combine all of the elements in Step 4 that can be used to customize a theme.

5 The selections for the customized theme are shown in the **Current theme** preview window

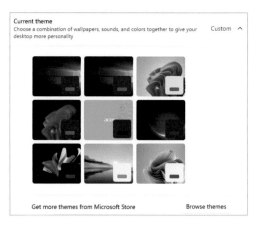

6   Click on the **Save** button to use it for the current theme

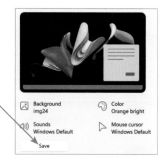

7   Click on one of the preset themes to select it rather than customizing one

8   Elements of the preset theme are displayed in the preview window

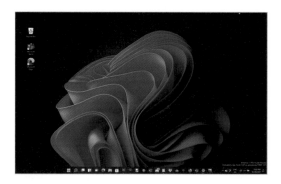

An internet connection is required to download more themes from the Microsoft Store.

9   Click on the **Browse themes** button in the **Get more themes from Microsoft Store** section to download more themes that can be used on your computer

Changing Color Themes

The Colors option in the Personalization section of the Settings app can be used to edit the overall color scheme of Windows 11, including a new Light theme that applies a crisper look and feel to all elements of the Windows 11 interface. To create this:

1 Open the **Settings** app and click on the **Personalization** tab

2 Click on the **Colors** option

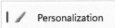

3 Click the drop-down menu in the **Choose your mode** section

4 Click on the **Light** option to apply a Light theme to the elements of Windows 11

5 The Light theme is also applied to the Start menu and the Taskbar

The Color themes do not alter the Desktop background. This is done in **Settings** > **Personalization** > **Background**.

6 If the **Dark** option is selected in Step 4, the background and foreground will be inverted

7 Click the drop-down menus in the **Choose your default Windows mode** section and the **Choose your default app mode** section to select specific settings. For instance, the Windows mode could be **Dark**, and the default app mode could be **Light**

The Dark theme for apps can be useful in the evening, or low-level lighting, as it can be more relaxing on the eyes when looking at content on the screen.

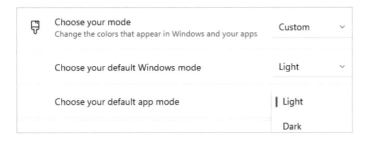

Lock Screen Settings

The Settings app enables you to set the appearance of the Lock screen and the Start menu, and to select an account photo. To do this, first access the Settings.

1 Open the **Settings** app and click on the **Personalization** tab

2 Click on the **Lock screen** option

3 The current Lock screen background is shown here

4 Click here to select options for the Lock screen background

5 Select one of the Lock screen background options from **Windows spotlight**, **Picture** or **Slideshow**

Don't forget

If **Slideshow** is selected in Step 5, you will then have the option to choose an album of photos to use as a slideshow for the Lock screen background.

6 For the Picture option, click on the **Browse photos** button to select your own picture

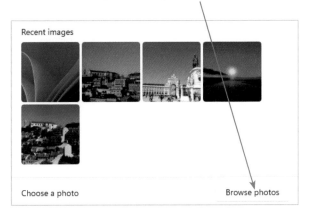

7 Select an image and click on **Choose picture** to add this to the background options for the Lock screen

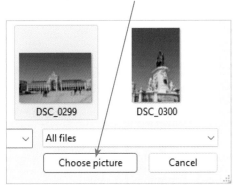

8 Other options for the Lock screen include selecting apps that display their detailed status on the Lock screen, and showing the Lock screen background image on the sign-in screen, as well as the Lock screen

Hot tip

If you use your own images for the Lock screen background, these will remain available on the thumbnail row even if you switch to another image for the background.

Changing Sounds

1 Select **Settings** >
Personalization > **Themes**

2 Click on the **Sounds** button
and you will see the following
dialog box open on the
Sounds tab

Click the Down arrow on
the **Sound Scheme**
drop-down bar to try
out a different scheme.

3 Select an option from the **Program Events** section
and click the **Test** button to hear the associated sound

If you do not want to
have sounds associated
with Windows events,
select **No Sounds** from
the options in the drop-
down list in Step 2.

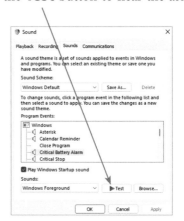

4 Browse to locate a new sound file (file type .wav), then
select **Test** to preview the effect

5 Make any other changes, then select **Save As...**, and
provide a name for your modified sound scheme

Desktop Icons

To control the display of icons on the Desktop:

1 Right-click on the Desktop, click **View** and select **Show desktop icons**. A check mark is added

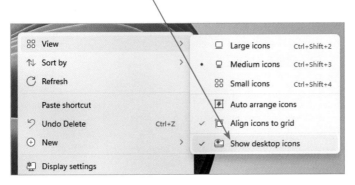

Hot tip

You can use the scroll wheel on your mouse to resize Desktop icons. On the Desktop, hold down **Ctrl** as you roll the wheel up or down.

2 To resize the icons, display the View menu as above and click **Large icons**, **Medium icons** or **Small icons**

3 To remove the check mark and hide all the icons, display the View menu and select **Show desktop icons** again

Hot tip

When you right-click the Desktop, you will find **Display settings** and **Personalize** customization functions on the context menu displayed.

4 To choose which of the system icons appear, open **Settings** and select **Personalization** > **Themes** > **Desktop icon settings** (under **Related settings**)

5 Select or clear the boxes to show or hide icons as required, then click **Apply** and **OK** to confirm the changes

Hot tip

The **Control Panel** is one of the options in Step 5, and a link to it can be added to the Desktop in this way.

Screen Resolution

If you have a high-resolution screen, you may find that the text, as well as the icons, is too small. You can increase the effective size by reducing the screen resolution.

If you want to use the Snap Assist function, as shown on pages 96-97, you need to have a minimum screen resolution of 1366 x 768.

1 Open the **Settings** app, select **System** and then click on the **Display** option

Display
Monitors, brightness, night light, display profile

2 Click here to change the screen resolution. Select a new resolution value from the list

Display resolution
Adjust the resolution to fit your connected display
1680 × 1050 (Recommended)

3 Click on a screen resolution, as required

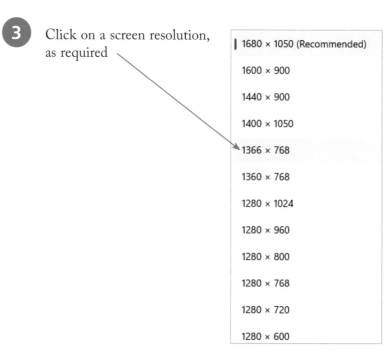

1680 × 1050 (Recommended)

1600 × 900

1440 × 900

1400 × 1050

1366 × 768

1360 × 768

1280 × 1024

1280 × 960

1280 × 800

1280 × 768

1280 × 720

1280 × 600

If you have an LCD monitor or a laptop computer, you are recommended to stay with the native resolution, normally the highest.

4 Click on the **Keep changes** button to change the screen resolution

Keep these display settings?

Reverting to previous display settings in 11 seconds.

Keep changes   Revert

Managing Storage

Computer storage is sometimes a feature that is taken for granted and left untouched. However, with Windows 11 there are some options for customizing how storage functions on your computer. To use these:

1 Open the **Settings** app, select **System** and then click on the **Storage** option

2 At the top of the window, the current storage is

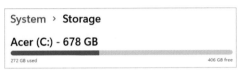

displayed, with the amount used shown by a colored bar

3 Drag the **Storage Sense** button **On** to enable Windows to free up storage space by deleting redundant files and items in the Recycle Bin

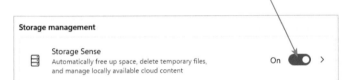

Most modern computers contain more than enough storage for most uses. However, it is useful to be able to see how much available storage there is and which apps are using the most storage.

4 The amount of storage space taken up by different types of content is displayed. Click on an item to view more details about it and manage its amount of storage space

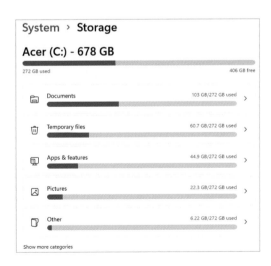

Accessibility

Making Windows 11 accessible for as wide a range of users as possible is an important consideration, and there are a range of accessibility settings that can be used for this. To do this:

The Accessibility settings have been renamed in Windows 11, from Ease of Access.

1 Open **Settings** and click on the **Accessibility** tab

2 Select options in the main panel

The settings for the Narrator can be used to specify items on the screen that are read out. For some items, such as buttons and controls, there is an audio description of the item.

3 Each option has settings that can be applied. For instance, drag the **Narrator** button from **Off** to **On** to enable items to be read out on the screen

There is also a Braille option that can be accessed toward the bottom of the Narrator window. This has to be used in conjunction with third-party software that communicates with a Braille display.

4 Select **Magnifier** in Step 2 on the previous page, and turn Magnifier **On** to activate the magnifying glass. Move this over areas of the screen to magnify them

In the **Magnifier** option, drag the **Invert colors** option **On** to highlight the area underneath the magnifier in inverted colors to the rest of the screen, to make it stand out more.

5 Select the **Contrast themes** option in Step 2 on the previous page and click in the **Contrast themes** box to select a color theme for text and background for users who find it difficult reading black text on a white background

Date and Time Functions

To change the format Windows uses to display dates and times:

1 Select the **Settings** > **Time & language** tab

| 🌐 Time & language

2 Click on the **Date & time** option

| 🕐 Date & time
| Time zones, automatic clock settings, calendar display

3 Drag the **Set time automatically** button **On** to enable the computer to set the time and date

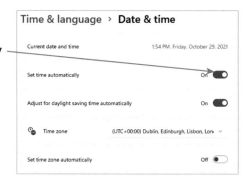

Time & language > **Date & time**

Current date and time	1:54 PM, Friday, October 29, 2021
Set time automatically	On ⬤
Adjust for daylight saving time automatically	On ⬤
🌐 Time zone	(UTC+00:00) Dublin, Edinburgh, Lisbon, Lon... ⌄
Set time zone automatically	Off ⬤

Don't forget

If the **Set time automatically** button is **Off**, click on the **Change** button next to the **Set the date and time manually** to set a manual date and time.

| Set the date and time manually | Change |

4 Click on the **Language & region** button to set the default geographical region for the computer

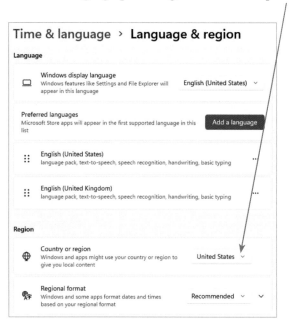

🌐 Language & region
Windows and some apps format dates and time based on your region

Time & language > **Language & region**

Language

🖥 Windows display language
Windows features like Settings and File Explorer will appear in this language
English (United States) ⌄

Preferred languages
Microsoft Store apps will appear in the first supported language in this list
Add a language

⠿ English (United States)
language pack, text-to-speech, speech recognition, handwriting, basic typing ⋯

⠿ English (United Kingdom)
language pack, text-to-speech, speech recognition, handwriting, basic typing ⋯

Region

🌐 Country or region
Windows and apps might use your country or region to give you local content
United States ⌄

🌐 Regional format
Windows and some apps format dates and times based on your regional format
Recommended ⌄ ⌄

6 File Explorer

File Explorer is at the heart of working with the files on your computer, and you can use it to browse all of the information on your computer and on the local network. This chapter shows how to use the File Explorer Menu bar, modify the views in File Explorer, use the Quick access folder, sort the contents, and customize its operation options.

Opening File Explorer

Although File Explorer is not necessarily one of the first apps that you will use with Windows 11, it still plays an important role in organizing your folders and files. To access File Explorer:

1 From the Desktop, click on this icon on the Taskbar; or

2 Press **WinKey** + **E**, and File Explorer opens at the **Quick access** folder

3 When File Explorer is opened, click on the **This PC** option to view the top-level items on your computer, including the main folders, your hard drive and any removable devices that are connected

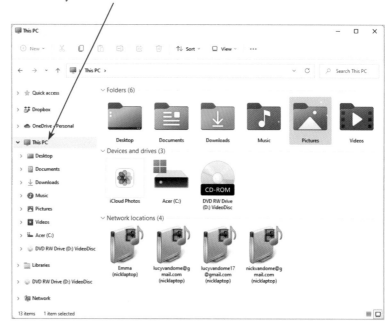

Beware

This PC displays files from different locations as a single collection, without actually moving any files.

Hot tip

You can click on the **Start** button and access File Explorer from here too.

File Explorer and the Taskbar

The Taskbar is visible at the bottom of the screen and displays thumbnails of the apps that have been added there. To illustrate the range of functions that it supports:

1 Open items are displayed on the Taskbar at the bottom of the window (denoted by a white or colored line underneath the item's icon – the color depends on your choices in the **Personalization** settings)

2 Right-click an open item on the Taskbar to view open files within the items and also recently viewed pages within it

The Taskbar is centered along the bottom of the screen by default in Windows 11, which is a new feature. If you prefer, you can change the setting so it is aligned to the left-hand side of the screen, as shown on page 47.

3 Move the mouse pointer over the File Explorer icon to see previews of open folder windows that File Explorer is managing (if File Explorer is open)

Libraries

File Explorer can use the Library for accessing the files and folders on your computer and network. Each Library displays files from several locations. Initially, there are five Libraries defined:

- **Camera Roll**, which is the default folder for photos captured on your computer (if it has a camera attached).

- **Documents**, which is the default folder for files such as those created with word processing or presentation apps.

- **Music**, which is the default folder for music bought from the online Microsoft Store, or added yourself.

- **Pictures**, which is the default folder for your photos.

- **Videos**, which is the default folder for your videos.

To view the Pictures Library, for example:

1 Select **Libraries > Pictures** in the Navigation pane

To add another folder to the Pictures Library:

1 Right-click in the Pictures Library window and select **New > Folder**

2 Click on the folder name and overwrite it with a new title

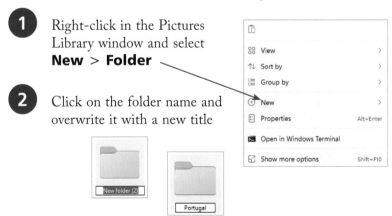

Beware

If photos are added to your computer from a USB flashdrive, rather than directly from a digital camera, then they will not be available in the Camera Roll.

124

File Explorer Menu Bar

The Menu bar in File Explorer has been simplified in Windows 11, replacing the Scenic Ribbon, but it can still be used for a variety of tasks for viewing and managing items within File Explorer.

1 The Menu bar is displayed at the top of File Explorer, regardless of which window is being viewed. If nothing is selected in File Explorer, a number of the options are unavailable (grayed out)

2 Click on an item within a File Explorer window to activate more of the options on the Menu bar

3 Click on the down-pointing arrow next to an item in the Menu bar to access its additional options

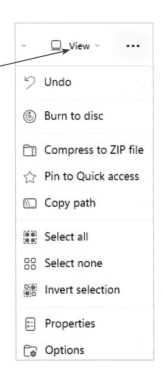

The File Explorer Menu bar has been updated in Windows 11.

Hot tip

Hover your mouse over the buttons to see the button names.

Don't forget

Right-click anywhere within a File Explorer window to access the File Explorer context menu; i.e. one that applies to the item in the current window.

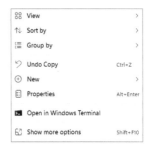

...cont'd

4 Click on the **New** button to view options for creating new files with specific apps, and also new folders and shortcuts to items within File Explorer

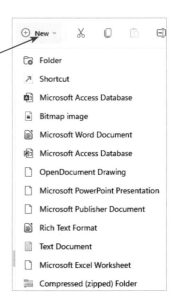

Don't forget

Click on the **View** button on the File Explorer Menu bar to select options for how the items in a File Explorer window are displayed.

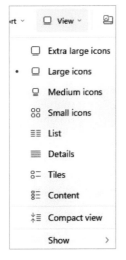

5 Depending on the content of a folder, different options are displayed on the Menu bar; e.g. if photos are selected, there are options specific to managing these

6 Select an item in a File Explorer window and click on the **Share** button to access options for sharing the selected item with other people, using email, social media, or online storage services

This PC Folder

One of the best ways to look at the contents of your computer involves using the This PC folder. To open this:

1 Open File Explorer and select **This PC** in the Navigation pane

Navigation pane   Location   Search box

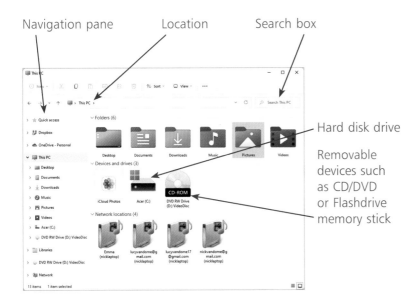

Hard disk drive

Removable devices such as CD/DVD or Flashdrive memory stick

The Navigation pane provides the facilities you require to move between folders and drives.

2 Select items and double-click to view their contents

Quick Access

When working with files and folders there will probably be items that you access on a regular basis. The Quick access section of File Explorer can be used to view the items that you have most recently accessed, and also to pin your most frequently used and favorite items. To use the Quick access section:

1 Click on the right-pointing arrow on the **Quick access** button in the File Explorer Navigation pane so that it becomes downward-pointing

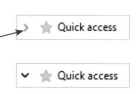

Items displayed under Quick access are not physically located there; the links are just shortcuts to the actual location within your file structure.

2 In the main window, your frequently used folders and most recently used files are displayed

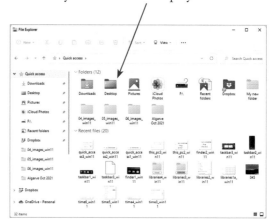

3 The folders are also listed underneath the **Quick access** button in the Navigation pane

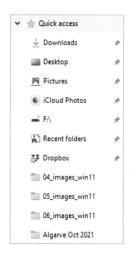

Adding items to Quick access

The folders that you access and use most frequently can be pinned to the Quick access section. This does not physically move them; it just creates a shortcut within Quick access. To do this:

1 Right-click on the folder you want to pin, and click on **Pin to Quick access**

2 The folder is pinned to the Quick access section, which is denoted by the pin symbol; or

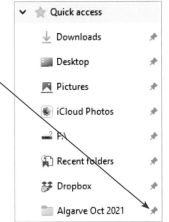

3 Drag the folder over the Quick access button until the **Pin to Quick access** option appears, and release

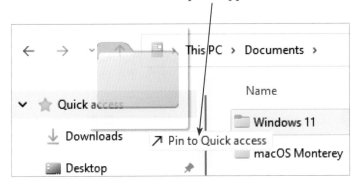

To unpin an item from Quick access, right-click on it and click on **Unpin from Quick access**.

Exploring Drives

Explore the contents of any drive from the This PC folder.

Flashdrives are also sometimes referred to as USB drives or USB devices.

1 Select one of the drive icons – for example, the **Flashdrive** removable storage device

Press the **Back arrow** (or **Forward arrow**, depending on how you have navigated in File Explorer) to go to the previous Library or location, or click the **Down arrow** to select from a list of viewed locations. Click the **Up arrow** to move up one level.

2 Double-click the **Flashdrive** device icon (or select it and press **Enter**) to display the files and folders that it contains

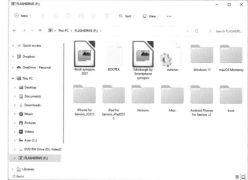

3 Double-click a folder entry (e.g. Windows 11) and select one of the files that it contains

4 Double-click the file icon and press **Enter** to open the file using the associated application

...cont'd

You can see all the folder entries in This PC in a structured list.

1 Double-click the **This PC** entry in the Navigation pane

2 The computer's folders are displayed, and the fixed drives plus any removable drives with media inserted are listed

You can also explore the folders in the **Quick access Libraries** and **Network** sections of attached computers.

3 Select the ❯ right-pointing arrow next to a heading level to expand that entry to the next level

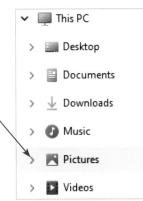

Resize the Navigation pane horizontally using the Stretch arrow, and traverse folder lists using the vertical scroll bar. See page 95 for more help with resizing panes/windows.

4 Select the ⌄ down-pointing arrow to collapse the entries to that heading level

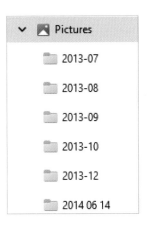

Address Bar

The Address bar at the top of File Explorer displays the current location as a set of names separated by arrows, and offers another way to navigate between Libraries and locations.

Don't forget

As you open more sub-folders within a File Explorer window, each sub-folder is added to the path in the Address bar, denoting the full file path of the selected folders. Selected files are not displayed in the Address bar.

1 To go to a location that is named in the address, click on that name in the Address bar; e.g. Documents

2 To select a sub-folder of a Library or location named in the Address bar, click on the arrow to the right

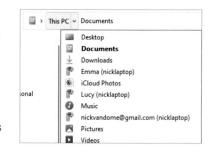

3 Click one of the entries to open it in place of the current location

When you are viewing a drive rather than a Library, the Address bar shows the drive and its folders, and allows you to navigate among these.

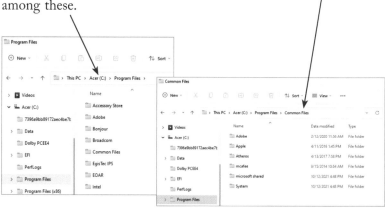

You can specify a new location using the Address bar.

1 Click on the Address bar in the blank space to the right of the set of names, and the full path is displayed

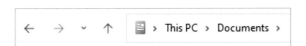

2 Type the complete folder path – e.g. C:\Users\Public (or click in the path and amend the values) – then press **Enter**

3 The specified location will be displayed

If you want a common location such as Desktop, just type the name alone and press **Enter**, and the location will be displayed:

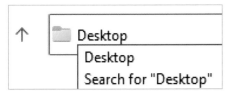

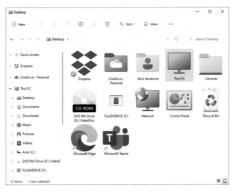

Hot tip

The path is highlighted by clicking in the Address bar, so typing a new path will completely replace the original item.

Hot tip

You can switch to exploring the internet by typing a web page address into the Address bar. The Microsoft Edge browser will be launched in a separate window.

Navigation Panes

The normal view for File Explorer includes the Navigation pane. There is also a Preview pane and a Details pane available.

You can choose different panes to display.

1 Open File Explorer and click on the **View** button

≡ View ˅   •••

☐ Extra large icons
☐ Large icons
🖵 Medium icons
🔡 Small icons
≣ List
≡ Details
▤ Tiles
▥ Content
‡≣ Compact view
Show   >

2 Click on the **Show** option

3 Click on the **Navigation pane** button to view this format. This appears down the left-hand side

✓ ▢ Navigation pane
  ▢ Details pane
  ▢ Preview pane
  🗹 Item check boxes
  📄 File name extensions
  👁 Hidden items

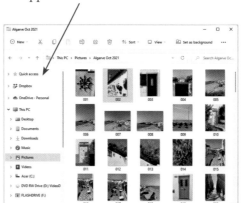

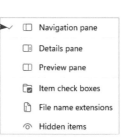

If you check **Off** the Navigation pane in Step 4, the left-hand panel will not be visible in File Explorer.

4 Click here to show or hide the Navigation pane. There are also options here for showing **Hidden items**

✓ ▢ Navigation pane
  ▢ Details pane
  ▢ Preview pane
  🗹 Item check boxes
  📄 File name extensions
  👁 Hidden items

5 Click on the **Preview pane** button to view a preview of the folder or file selected in the main window

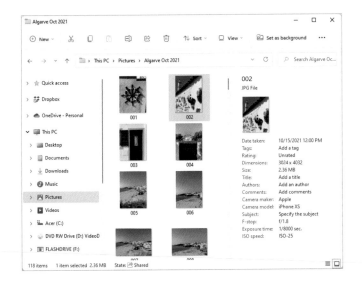

The Preview pane is particularly useful if you are working in the Pictures Library.

6 Click on the **Details pane** button to view additional information about the folder or file selected in the main window

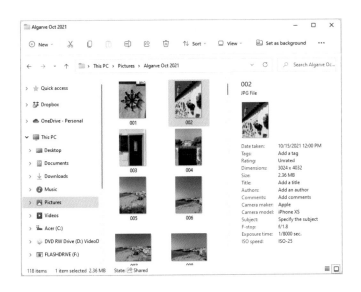

Changing Views

You can change the size and appearance of the file and folder icons in your folders, using the View button on the File Explorer Menu bar.

1 Open the folder you would like to change and click on the **View** button on the File Explorer Menu bar. Select one of the options for viewing content in the folder

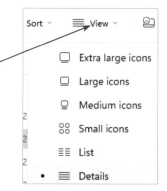

2 Click on different items to change the appearance of icons

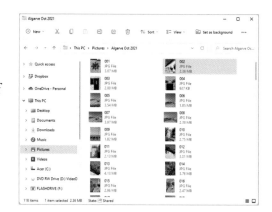

3 Hover the cursor over each **View** setting to preview. Click the mouse button to apply that view

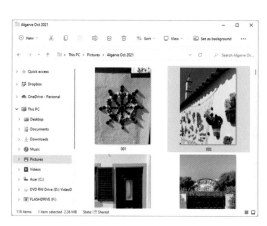

Sorting

Windows 11 allows you to sort your files in a drive or folder by various attributes or descriptors.

1 Open a folder, click on **View** > **Details** and select the attribute header that you want to sort by; e.g. Date

2 The entries are sorted in ascending order by the selected attribute. The header includes a sort symbol ∧

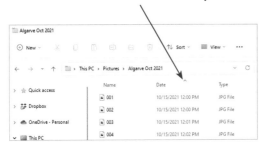

3 Select the header again. The order is reversed and the header now shows an inverted sort symbol ∨

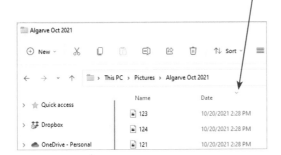

4 The contents will remain sorted in the selected sequence, even if you switch to a different folder view

Don't forget

Right-click on a column heading in Steps 2 and 3 to select which column headings appear; e.g. Date, Size, Type, etc.

Hot tip

Note that any sub-folders within your folder will be sorted to the end of the list when you reverse the sequence. Libraries are an exception and keep folders at the top (in the appropriate sort order).

Filtering

1 In the Details view (see page 135), select any header and click the **Down arrow** to the right-hand side

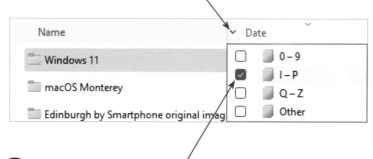

2 Select a box next to one or more ranges, and the items displayed are immediately restricted to that selection

3 You can select a second header – **Size**, for example – to apply additional filtering to the items displayed

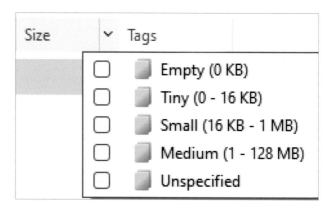

4 The check mark ✓ symbol on headers indicates that filtering is in effect, and the Address bar shows the attributes

5 Filtering remains in effect even if you change folder views within the selected folder

Grouping

You can group the contents of a folder using header ranges. You do not need to select Details view.

1 Right-click an empty part of the folder area, select **Group by**, then select an attribute; e.g. **Size**

The right-click context menu also offers the **Sort by** option so that you can specify or change the sort sequence without switching to Details view.

2 The contents will be grouped, using the ranges for the attribute selected

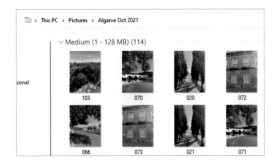

Any sorting that was already in place will remain in effect. However, you can switch between **Ascending** and **Descending**.

3 Grouping is retained when you switch views (and when you revisit the folder after closing File Explorer)

Select **Group by** > **(None)** to remove grouping. Select **More** to add other attributes. The new attributes will also appear in Details view.

4 You can regroup the folder contents by selecting another attribute. This will replace your original choice

Folder Options

You can change the appearance and the behavior of your folders by adjusting the folder settings.

1 From the **See more** button on the File Explorer Menu bar, click on the **Options** button

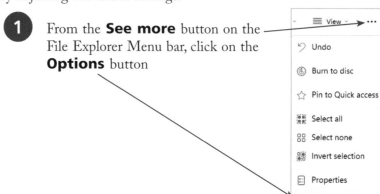

The same dialog box is displayed if you access **Control Panel** > **Appearance and Personalization** (from the Category view), then select **File Explorer Options**.

2 Choose **Open each folder in the same window**, to keep multiple folders open at the same time

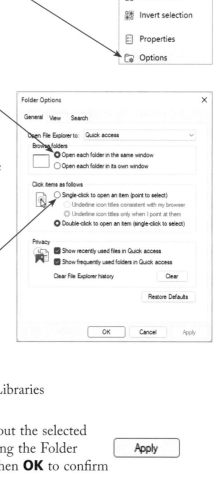

3 If you want items to open as they do on a web page, select **Single-click to open an item (point to select)**

To open a sub-folder in its own window, when **Open each folder in the same window** is set, right-click the sub-folder and select **Open in new window**.

4 Select the **View** tab to select options for how items appear in the File Explorer Libraries

5 Select **Apply** to try out the selected changes without closing the Folder Options dialog box, then **OK** to confirm

Apply

6 Alternatively, select **Restore Defaults** then **Apply**, to reset all options to their default values

Restore Defaults

7 Managing Files and Folders

This chapter shows how to manage folders and files within File Explorer, including moving, copying, and deleting items, and also searching for folders and files within File Explorer. It also shows how to use the Recycle Bin and view file properties to see as much detail about them as possible.

Selecting Files and Folders

To process several files or folders, it is more efficient to select and process them as a group, rather than one by one.

Single file or folder

1 Click an item to highlight it, then move, copy or delete it as required

Sequential files

1 To highlight a range, click to select the first item, press and hold **Shift**, then click the last item

Adjacent block

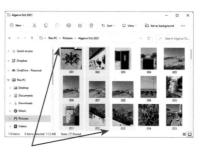

1 Click and drag a box to cover the files you want selected. All the files in the rectangular area will be highlighted

Use the sorting, filtering and grouping options (see pages 137-139) to rearrange files to make selection easier.

You must start a selection box from an empty space in a folder. If you accidentally click a file or folder, you will drag that item, rather than create a box.

...cont'd

Non-adjacent files

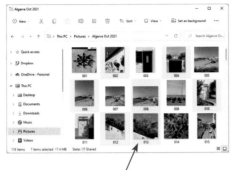

1 To select several non-adjacent files, click one item, press and hold **Ctrl**, then click the subsequent items. As you select files, they are highlighted

Partial sequence

You can combine these techniques to select part of a range.

1 Select a group of sequential files or an adjacent block of files (as described on the previous page)

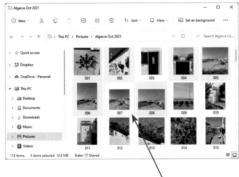

2 Hold down **Ctrl** and click to deselect any files in the range that you do not want, and to select extra ones

All files and folders

To select all of the files (and folders) in the current folder, click on the **Menu** button on the File Explorer Menu bar and click on **Select All** or press **Ctrl** + **A**.

Hot tip

To deselect one file, click it while the **Ctrl** key is being held down. To deselect all of the files, click once anywhere in the folder outside of the selection area.

143

Beware

If you select a folder, you will also be selecting any files and folders that it may contain.

Copying or Moving Files or Folders

You may wish to copy or move files and folders to another folder on the same drive, or to another drive. There are several ways to achieve this.

Drag, using the right mouse button

1 Open File Explorer and the folder with the required files, then locate the destination in the **Folders** list in the Navigation pane

Hot tip

Select an item in a File Explorer window, right-click on it and click on this button on the menu that appears to copy it:

144

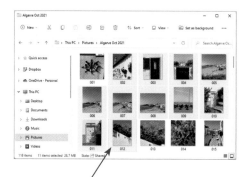

2 In the folder contents, select the files and folders that you want to copy or move

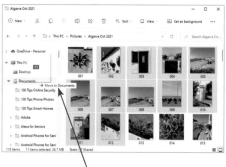

3 Right-click any one of the selection, drag the files onto the destination folder or drive in the **Folders** list so that it is highlighted and named, then release to display the menu

4 Click the **Move here** or **Copy here** option as desired, and the files will be added to the destination folder

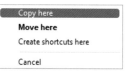

...cont'd

Drag, using the left mouse button

In this case, default actions are applied with no intervening menu.

1 Select files and folders to be moved or copied

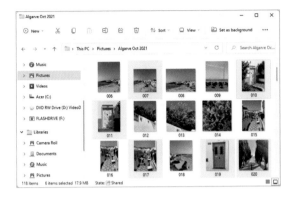

Hot tip

Open File Explorer and the source folder, then locate the destination in the **Folders** list in the Navigation pane, ready for moving or copying files and folders.

2 Use the left mouse button to drag the selection to the destination drive or folder in the **Folders** list – in this example, the removable USB storage drive (Flashdrive)

3 Press **Shift** to Move instead of Copy to another drive. Press **Ctrl** to Copy instead of Move to a folder on the same drive as the source folder

Don't forget

You will see a **+** symbol if the file is going to be copied, or a **→** symbol if the file is going to be moved.

In summary

Drives	Drag	Drag + Shift	Drag + Ctrl
Same	Move	Move	Copy
Different	Copy	Move	Copy

...cont'd

Using Cut, Copy and Paste

In the File Explorer context menu in Step 2, the most commonly used options – e.g. **Cut**, **Copy**, **Rename**, **Share** and **Delete** – are displayed as icons at the top of the menu, rather than as text. This is a new feature in Windows 11.

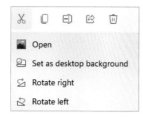

Click the **Show more options** button at the bottom of this menu (see image in Step 2), to display the full list of options that you might be more used to from older versions of Windows.

Hot tip

Cut does not remove the selection initially – it just dims it until you **Paste** it (see Step 5). Press **Esc** if you decide to cancel the move, and the item will remain in place.

1 Choose files and folders you want to copy, and right-click within the selection

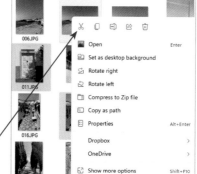

2 From the context menu, click **Copy** or **Cut** to move the selection

3 Move to the destination folder (or create a new one)

4 Right-click a blank area of the destination folder

5 Select **Paste** from the menu to complete the copy or move operation

Keyboard shortcuts

Cut, Copy and Paste options are also available as keyboard shortcuts. Select files and folders as above, but use these keys in place of the menu selections for Copy, Cut and Paste. There are also shortcuts to Undo an action or Redo an action.

Press this key	To do this
F1	Display Help
Ctrl+C	Copy the selected item
Ctrl+X	Cut the selected item
Ctrl+V	Paste the selected item
Ctrl+Z	Undo an action
Ctrl+Y	Redo an action

Burn to disc

If your computer has a CD or DVD recorder, you can copy files to a writable disc. This is usually termed "burning".

1 Insert a writable (or re-writable) CD or DVD disc into the recorder drive (DVD/CD RW)

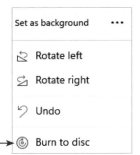

Set as background   •••

🔃 Rotate left

🔁 Rotate right

↩ Undo

◎ Burn to disc

2 Open File Explorer and select files or folders as required. Click on the **Menu** button and click on the **Burn to disc** option

3 If no disc has already been inserted, you will be prompted to do so

Burn to Disc   ✕

Insert a disc

Please insert a writable disc into drive D:.

Help me choose a disc

Cancel

Another, more modern, option for copying files and folders from your computer is to use a USB flashdrive, which shows up as an external drive in File Explorer when it is inserted.

147

4 The selected files are displayed in the DVD (or CD) drive in File Explorer

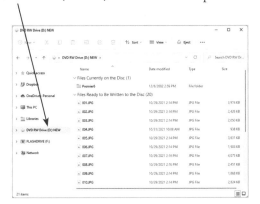

You can use any of the methods described for copying or moving one or more files and folders.

5 Click on the **Menu** button in File Explorer and click on **Burn to disc** again to burn the selected files or folders to the disc

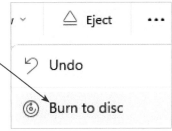

⏏ Eject   •••

↩ Undo

◎ Burn to disc

File Conflicts

When you copy or move files from one folder to another, conflicts may arise. There may already be a file with the same name in the destination folder. To illustrate what may happen:

1 Open a folder (e.g. **Documents** > **Windows 11** folder) and the USB flashdrive

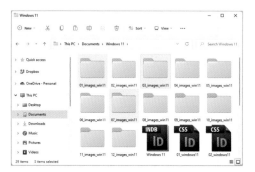

2 Press **Ctrl** + **A** to select all of the files and drag them onto the flashdrive, to initiate a copy of them

3 Windows observes any conflicts – some files already exist, with identical size and date information. Select one of the options

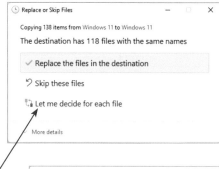

4 If you select the **Let me decide for each file** option, details will be displayed so that you can view if one is newer than another. Click on the **Continue** button to confirm the decisions made

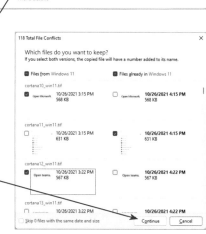
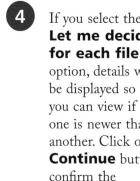

You can, of course, use the Copy and Paste options from the right-click menus, or use the equivalent keyboard shortcuts, and File Explorer will continue to check for possible conflicts.

Opening Files

You can open a file using an associated app without first having to explicitly start that app. There are several ways to do this.

Default program

1 Double-click the file icon; or

2 Right-click the file and select **Open** from the menu

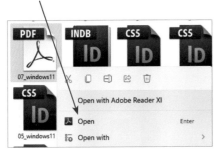

Default programs can also be set in **Settings** > **Apps** > **Default apps** (scroll to the bottom of the screen to find options to choose defaults by file type or to reset defaults) or **Control Panel** > **Programs** > **Default programs** (in Category view).

Alternative program (app)

You may have several apps that can open a particular file type. To use a different app than the default to open the file:

1 Right-click the file icon and select **Open with**. Pick an app from the list or click **Choose another app** to set a new default app

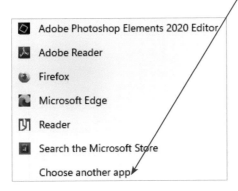

2 The same choices are presented when you select the Down arrow next to the **Open** button on the Ribbon in the folder window

Deleting Files and Folders

When you want to remove files or folders, you use the same delete procedures – whichever drive or device the items are stored on.

1 Choose one or more files and folders, selected as described previously (see pages 142-143)

2 Right-click the selection and click **Delete**

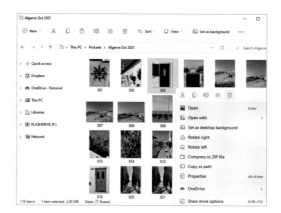

Don't forget

When you delete files and folders from your hard disk drive, they are actually moved to a temporary storage area: the Recycle Bin (see pages 151-153).

3 Alternatively, click on the **Delete** button on the Menu bar

If you choose to delete and then immediately realize that you have made a mistake deleting one or more files, right-click the folder area and select **Undo Delete** or press **Ctrl** + **Z**, to reverse the last operation. For hard disk items, you are also able to retrieve deleted files from the Recycle Bin, and this could be a substantial time later (unless you have emptied or bypassed the Recycle Bin – see pages 152-153).

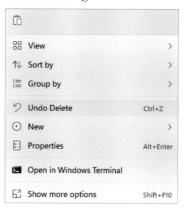

Hot tip

You can press the **Delete** key on your keyboard after selecting files and folders, instead of using the File Explorer Menu bar.

The Recycle Bin

The Recycle Bin is, in effect, a folder on your hard disk that holds deleted files and folders. They are not physically removed from your hard disk (unless you empty the Recycle Bin or delete specific items from within the Recycle Bin itself). They will remain there until the Recycle Bin fills up, at which time the oldest deleted files may finally be removed.

The Recycle Bin, therefore, provides a safety net for files and folders you may delete by mistake, and allows you to easily retrieve them, even at a later date.

Restoring files

1 Double-click on the **Recycle Bin** icon from the Desktop or in the Navigation pane

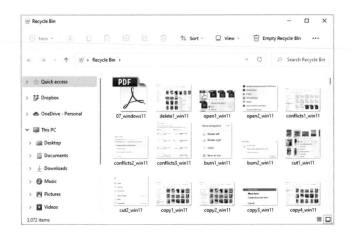

2 Select the **Restore all items** button, or select a file and the button changes to **Restore the selected items**

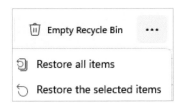

Hot tip

A restored folder will include all the files and sub-folders that it held when it was originally deleted.

...cont'd

Permanently erase files

You may want to explicitly delete particular files, perhaps for reasons of privacy and confidentiality.

1 Open the Recycle Bin

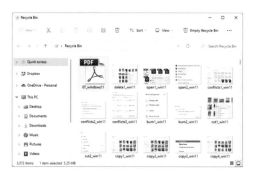

2 Select the relevant files and folders and click on the **Delete** button on the Menu bar

3 Select **Yes**, to confirm that you want to permanently delete these files (completely remove them from the hard disk)

Empty the Recycle Bin

If desired, you can remove all of the contents of the Recycle Bin from the hard disk.

1 With the Recycle Bin open, select the **Empty Recycle Bin** button

2 Press **Yes** to confirm the permanent deletion

The Recycle Bin icon changes from full to empty, to illustrate the change.

Don't forget

You do not have to worry about the space used in the Recycle Bin. Windows keeps track and removes the oldest deleted entries when the maximum allowed space – typically 10% of the drive – has been used.

Bypass the Recycle Bin

If you want to prevent particular deleted files from being stored in the Recycle Bin:

1 From their original location, select files and folders, right-click the selection, but this time hold down the **Shift** key as you select the **Delete** button

2 Confirm that you want to permanently delete the selected item or items. "Permanent" means that no copy will be kept

Deactivate (or resize) the Recycle Bin

You can tell Windows to always bypass the Recycle Bin.

1 Right-click the Recycle Bin icon, then select **Properties** from the menu

2 Note the space available in the Recycle Bin location (free space on hard disk)

3 Adjust the maximum size allowed, to resize the Recycle Bin

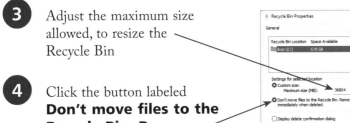

4 Click the button labeled **Don't move files to the Recycle Bin. Remove files immediately when deleted.**, to always bypass the Recycle Bin

Creating a Folder

You can create a new folder in a drive, folder or on the Desktop.

1 Right-click an empty part of the folder window, select **New** and then **Folder**

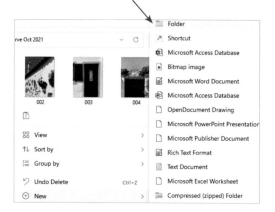

Make sure that you click in the space between icons, away from (usually hidden) boxes surrounding icons.

2 Overtype the default name **New Folder** and press **Enter** on the keyboard

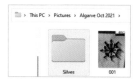

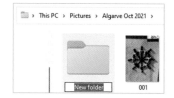

If you click away from an icon without typing the new name, you get folders called **New Folder**, **New Folder (2)**, and so on.

You can also create a new file in a standard format for use with one of the apps installed on your computer.

1 Right-click an empty part of the folder, select **New**, and choose a specific file type; e.g. Text Document file

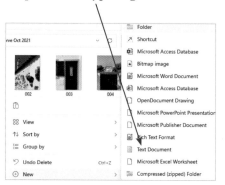

Normally, the file name extension (which shows the file type) will be hidden. To reveal file extensions, select **View** > **Show** from the File Explorer Menu bar and check **On** the **File name extensions** box.

Renaming a File or Folder

You can rename a file or folder at any time, by simply editing the current name.

1 Right-click the file/folder, then click the **Rename** button, or select it from the Menu bar

155

Hot tip

Use the same method to rename icons on the Desktop. You can even rename the Recycle Bin.

2 Either way, the current name will be highlighted. Type a name to delete and replace the current name, or press the arrow keys to position the typing cursor and edit the existing name

Don't forget

You must always provide a non-blank file name, and you should avoid special characters such as quote marks, question marks and periods/full stops.

3 Press **Enter** on the keyboard or click elsewhere to confirm the new name

Preserving file types

When you have file extensions revealed and you create or rename a file or folder, only the name itself, not the file type, will be highlighted. This avoids accidental changes of type.

Beware

You can change the file type (extension), but you will be warned that this may make the file unusable.

Backtracking File Operations

If you accidentally delete, rename, copy or move the wrong file or folder, you can undo (reverse) the last operation and preceding operations, to get back to where you started. For example:

Hot tip

Undo mistakes as soon as possible, since you would have to undo subsequent operations first. Also, only a limited amount of undo history is maintained.

1 Right-click the folder area and select the **Undo Rename** command that is displayed

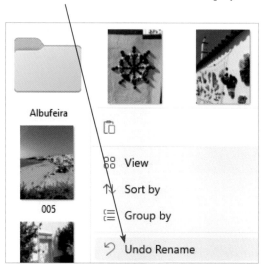

Don't forget

The **Undo** command that is offered changes depending on which operation was being performed at the time.

2 Right-click again, and click on the **Undo Delete** command

Don't forget

If you go back too far, right-click the folder and select the available Redo operation; e.g. Redo Rename.

3 Now, you will have reversed the last two operations, putting the folder and files back as they were before the changes

Beware

Undo commands do not work on permanently deleted files.

File Properties

Every file (and every folder) has information that can be displayed in the Properties dialog box. To display this:

1 Right-click the file or folder icon to display the shortcut menu

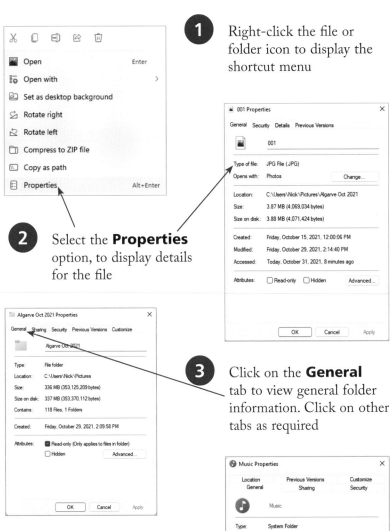

2 Select the **Properties** option, to display details for the file

3 Click on the **General** tab to view general folder information. Click on other tabs as required

4 Similarly, you can display properties for any of the Libraries

Hot tip

The purpose of the **Properties** dialog box is:
• to display details;
• to change settings for the selected file or folder.

Don't forget

Click **Security** and the other tabs to display more information about a file or folder, and click the **Advanced** button for additional attributes.

Searching for Files and Folders

If you are not quite sure where exactly you stored a file, or what the full name is, the File Explorer Search box may be the answer.

1 Open a location – e.g. Documents – click in the Search box and start typing a word from the file; e.g. *Nick*

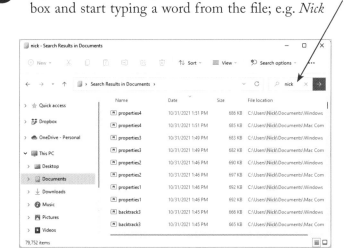

2 If that produces too many files, start typing another word that might help limit the number of matches; e.g. *Vandome*

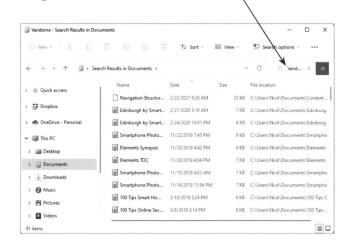

3 If the location is a drive rather than a Library, its contents may not be indexed, so the search may take longer

Hot tip

Open the Library or folder that is most likely to hold the file you want, then click in the Search box to initiate a search, looking at file names and content limited to that folder and its sub-folders.

Don't forget

Some files contain search words in the file names, while others contain words within the textual content.

Hot tip

For an attached hard drive, you may be offered the option to **Click to add to index**, and thereby speed up future searches. Indexing is the process of the Search facility storing words that can be searched over.

Hot tip

You can also use Cortana to search for files and folders.

Compressed Folders

This feature allows you to save disk space by compressing files and folders, while allowing them to be treated as normal by Windows 11.

Create a compressed folder

1 Right-click an empty portion of the folder window and select **New > Compressed (zipped) Folder**

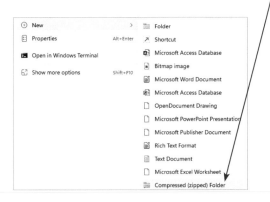

Hot tip

Compressed folders are distinguished from other folders by a zipper on the folder icon. They are compatible with other zip archive apps, such as WinZip.

Algarve Oct 2021

2 A compressed folder is created, with a .zip extension

Algarve Oct

3 The compressed file can be renamed if required (see page 155) and also opened moved or deleted like another folder

Add files or folders to a compressed folder

1 Drag files or folders onto a compressed folder and they will automatically be compressed and stored there

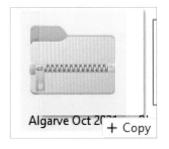

Algarve Oct 2... + Copy

Don't forget

To create a compressed folder and copy a file into it at the same time, right-click a file in File Explorer and select **Compress to ZIP file**. The new compressed folder has the same file name, but with a file extension of .zip.

...cont'd

Compressed item properties

1 Double-click the compressed folder and select any file to see the compressed size versus the original size

Extract files and folders

1 Open the compressed folder, drag files and folders onto a normal folder, and they will be decompressed. The compressed version still remains in the compressed folder, unless you hold the **Shift** key as you drag (i.e. Move)

Extract all

1 To extract all of the files and folders from a compressed folder, right-click it and then click on **Extract all**

2 Accept or edit the target folder and click **Extract**. The files and folders are decompressed and transferred

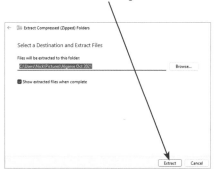

Hot tip

If a folder specified does not exist, it will be created automatically.

8 Digital Lifestyle

Windows 11 covers a range of entertainment with the Photos, Groove Music and Movies & TV apps. This chapter shows how to work with these apps, and also the online OneDrive function for backing up content.

Using OneDrive

Cloud computing is now a mainstream part of our online experience. This involves saving content to an online server connected to the service that you are using – i.e. through your Microsoft Account. You can then access this content from any computer or mobile device using your account login details, and also share it with other people by giving them access to your cloud service. It can also be used to back up your files, in case they get corrupted or damaged on your computer.

The cloud service with Windows 11 is known as OneDrive, and you can use it with a Microsoft Account. It consists of the OneDrive folder in File Explorer, the OneDrive app, and the online OneDrive website. Content added to any of the elements will be available in the others. To use them:

Don't forget

OneDrive has a **Personal Vault** folder that has added levels of security for storing your most sensitive and important documents and photos. It requires an extra level of security to access the Personal Vault; e.g. a PIN code or a code that is sent to you via email or text message. The Personal Vault can be accessed from any of the OneDrive interfaces.

1 Click on the **OneDrive** folder in File Explorer to view its contents. Or, click on this button on the Start menu

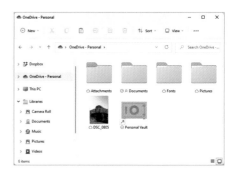

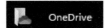

2 Download the OneDrive app from the Microsoft Store and click on this icon  on the Start menu to open it. It should display the same items as in the OneDrive folder in File Explorer

Don't forget

Click on these buttons on the right-hand side of the OneDrive toolbar in Step 2 (i.e. when you are signed in to the web version of OneDrive) to, from left to right: sort the content; display it as a grid; or view its details:

3 To view the contents of
OneDrive online, go to
the website at **onedrive.
live.com** and sign in
with your Microsoft
Account details. Your
OneDrive content is
the same as in your
OneDrive folder on your computer

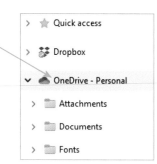

Your OneDrive folder
can be pinned to the
Quick access section
in File Explorer. To do
this, right-click on the
OneDrive icon in File
Explorer and click on
Pin to Quick access.

Files and folders can be added to OneDrive from any of the three
elements.

Adding items to OneDrive in File Explorer

1 In File Explorer, the OneDrive
folder is located below Quick
access (and any other folders
that have been added)

2 Click on the OneDrive
folder to view its contents

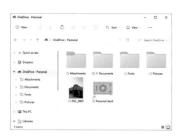

By default, you get 5GB
of free OneDrive storage
space with Windows 11
(the free allowance was
reduced from 15GB in
July 2016). This is an
excellent way to back
up your important
documents, since they
are stored away from
your computer. For
up-to-date information
on plan allowances and
pricing, visit **https://
onedrive.live.com/
about/plans/**

3 Add files to the OneDrive
folder by dragging and
dropping them from
another folder, or by using
Copy and Paste

163

...cont'd

Adding items to the OneDrive app

1 Open the OneDrive app and click on the **Upload** button

2 Select whether to upload **Files** or a **Folder** from your computer

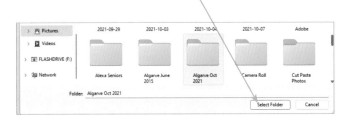

3 Navigate to the required item in File Explorer, select it, and click on the **Select Folder** button to add it to your OneDrive folder

Adding items to OneDrive online

1 Access your online OneDrive account and click on the **Upload** button

2 Select whether to upload **Files** or a **Folder** and navigate to the required items as above

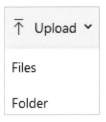

OneDrive Settings

A range of settings can be applied to OneDrive, including adding and syncing folders. To do this:

1 Right-click on the OneDrive icon on the Notifications area of the Taskbar and click on **Settings**

2 Click on the **Settings** tab for options for starting OneDrive when you sign in, and for receiving notifications if other people share items to your OneDrive account

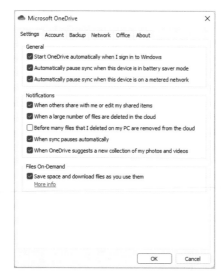

3 Click on the **Account** tab and click on the **Choose folders** button to select a folder from your computer that you want to sync with your OneDrive account

4 Click on the **OK** button to apply any changes to the OneDrive settings

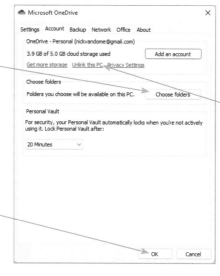

> **Don't forget**
>
> If the OneDrive icon is not visible on the Taskbar, access it in the **All apps** section of the Start menu, right-click on it and click on **Pin to taskbar**.

> **Don't forget**
>
> The Account section can also be used to unlink your PC so that files on your computer are not synced with the online OneDrive. Click on the **Unlink this PC** option to do this.

Viewing Photos

The Photos app can be used to manage and edit your photos, including those stored in your **Pictures** Library. To do this:

Hot tip

To import photos into the Photos app, click on this button on the top toolbar and select a location from where you want to import the photos. This can be a folder on your own computer; a camera or flashdrive attached with a USB cable; or a memory card from a camera inserted into a card reader.

1 Click on the **Photos** app on the Start menu or the Taskbar

2 The main categories are at the left-hand side of the screen, on the top toolbar

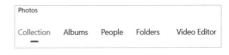

3 Other options are at the right-hand side of the toolbar

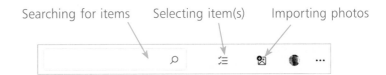

Searching for items   Selecting item(s)   Importing photos

Hot tip

Click on the **People** button in Step 2 to use facial technology to identify people in your photos. Click on the **Video Editor** button to access options for creating video projects.

4 Click on the **Collection** button to view all of the photos in the Photos app, arranged by date. Scroll up and down to view the photos

Don't forget

Click on the **Folders** button in Step 2 to view photos that have been taken with your computer's camera (or copied into this folder from another location).

5 Click on the **Albums** button to view photos from specific albums

6 Within the Albums section, double-click on an album to view its contents. The first photo is also displayed as a banner at the top of the album

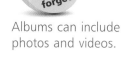

Albums can include photos and videos.

7 Double-click on a photo within an album or collection to view it at full size, with the toolbar shown at the top of the window

Photos within either a collection or an album in the Photos app can be selected and then shared with other people in various ways, or deleted. To do this: in Collection or an open album, click on the **Select** button on the top toolbar.

Click in the box in the top-right corner to select a photo or photos. Click on the **Share** button to share the selected photo(s).

Editing Photos

In Windows 11, the Photos app has a range of editing functions so that you can improve and enhance your photos. To use these:

1 Open a photo at full size, with the top toolbar displayed

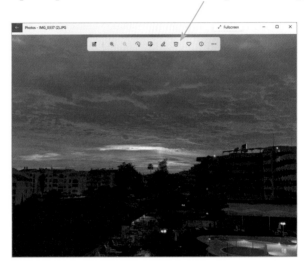

Hot tip

Move the cursor over the items on the top toolbar in Step 1 to view a description about each of the buttons.

2 Click on the **Edit image** button on the top toolbar. Click on these buttons to view the editing options

Edit image (Ctrl+E)

Hot tip

The **Draw** button is available from the toolbar. Click on this to access pen options for drawing directly on an image. Click on the **Save** button to save a copy of the image, or click on the cross to discard changes.

Draw

3 By default, the **Crop & rotate** option is opened in Step 2 on the previous page. This can be used to crop the current photo or rotate it in a variety of ways, such as straightening, or flipping horizontally or vertically

4 Click on the **Filters** button from the editing options to apply filter effects. Click on an effect to apply it to the photo

5 Click on the **Adjustments** button from the editing options to apply a range of color adjustments. Click next to an adjustment category to view more options. Drag the sliders to apply the amount of the editing option, as required

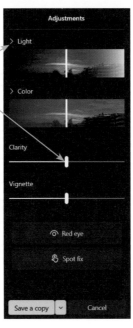

Most photos benefit from some degree of cropping, so that the main subject is given greater prominence by removing unwanted items in the background.

169

Click on the **Save a copy** button at the bottom of the editing panel to save a copy of an edited image, without changing the original. Click on the down-pointing arrow to access an option to **Save** the edited image, which now becomes the original.

Groove Music

The Groove Music app is used to access music that you have added to your computer. To use it:

1 Click on the **Groove Music** app on the Start menu

2 Click on the **Menu** button to expand the menu so that the titles are visible, not just the icons

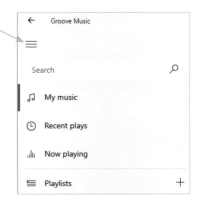

3 Click on a category to view those items; e.g. **My music** for the music that you have available on your computer

4 Items within the selected category are displayed. Use the tabs on the top toolbar to view items according to these categories

Playing Music

Playing your own music

Music that has been added to your computer can be played through the Groove Music app, and you can automatically specify new music to be included when it is added. To do this:

1 Open the Groove Music app and click on the **My music** button

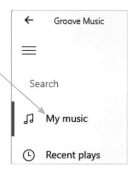

You can also add music to the Groove Music app from the Library that you have stored in your OneDrive folder.

2 Click on **Songs**, **Artists** or **Albums** tabs, as shown in Step 4 on the previous page, to view the items within each category

When a folder is added to the Music Library, any music that is copied there will be displayed by the Groove Music app.

3 Click on an item to access it

4 Click on a track or album to start playing it

5 Use these buttons below to, from left to right: shuffle the available tracks; go to the start of a track; pause/play a track; go to the end of a track; repeat a track; or change or mute the volume

The Spotify app can be used to stream music using Windows 11. This can be downloaded from the Microsoft Store.

Viewing Movies and TV

For movie and TV lovers, the Movies & TV app can be used to download and watch your favorite movies and shows. It connects to the Microsoft Store from where you can preview and buy a large range of content.

The Movies & TV app is called **Films & TV** in some regions.

Click on the **Purchased** button in Step 2 to view all of the items you have bought.

Movies and TV shows can be streamed (viewed from the computer server where the item is stored, rather than downloading it) if you have a fast internet connection. They can also be downloaded to a single device so that they can be viewed while you are offline.

1 Click on the **Movies & TV** app on the Start menu

2 The Microsoft Store opens at the **Explore** section for viewing available items

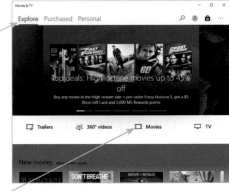

3 Click on the **Movies** (or **TV**) button to view the available items

4 Click on an item to see more information, view a preview clip, or buy or rent a movie

5 Click on the **Trailers** button in Step 3 on the previous page to view previews of movies

6 Click on an item to view its trailer

7 The trailer plays in the Movies & TV window

The interface for viewing a trailer is the same as for viewing a movie or TV show that has been bought or rented. Click on the main window to access the control buttons at the bottom of the screen.

173

8 Click on the **Personal** button on the top toolbar to view your own videos that have been added to your computer. Items from the **Video** folders are displayed, and new folders can be added, using the **Add folders** button

Personal

Using Paint 3D

Windows 11 caters for a wide range of 3D use, and one of the most significant apps is the Paint 3D app that can be used to create your own 3D pictures using graphics and text, and also to import ones from other places.

Around Paint 3D

In some ways, Paint 3D is an extension of the Windows Paint app. However, it has a much greater array of features, and brings the creation of 3D pictures within reach of anyone. To get started with creating 3D pictures:

1 Click on the **Paint 3D** app

2 Click on the **New** button to create a new blank project

3 The Paint 3D workspace includes the canvas (the white square in the middle), the background, tools for creating content, and the tools palette (at the right-hand side)

4 Click on the **Brushes** button on the top toolbar to select brush types and colors

5 Click on the **3D shapes** button on the top toolbar to add 3D shapes

6 Click on the **Stickers** button on the top toolbar to add 3D graphics

7 Click on the **Text** button on the top toolbar to add 3D text effects

8 Click on the **Effects** button on the top toolbar to add background effects

Gaming with Windows 11

Game players are well catered for in Windows 11, with the Xbox Console Companion app for playing games and interacting with other gamers. To play games with Windows 11:

1 Click on the **Start** button and click on the **Xbox Console Companion** app

2 Click on the **Home** button to view the Xbox Homepage. This contains the **Toolbar** (down the left-hand side), the **Activity feed** (in the middle panel) and options for joining clubs and connecting with other gamers (in the right-hand panel)

You have to be signed in with your Microsoft Account in order to use the Xbox Console Companion app and all of its features.

3 Click on the **My games** button to view system games or those that you have downloaded from the Microsoft Store

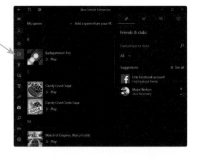

Click on the **Play** button next to a game in Step 3 to open it and start playing it.

4 Click on the **Achievements** button to view your scores from games you have played, and compare them with other gamers

...cont'd

Click on this button on the toolbar to view any screenshots or videos that you have captured of the games you have played. This can be done with the **Game Bar**, which can be opened by pressing **WinKey** + **G**:

Click on this button on the toolbar to view **Trending** topics from within the gaming community:

Using the Xbox Console Companion app with Windows 11 can be a very interactive experience in terms of communicating with and playing with other gamers. However, it can also be used to play games on your own.

5. Click on the **Clubs** button to view details of online game-playing clubs. This is where you can join up with other players, to compare scores and also play online games against other players (multiplayer games)

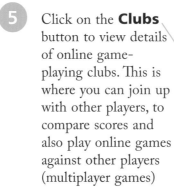

6. In the right-hand panel, click on the **Friends list** button to view friends that you have added (this can be done by searching for them through the Xbox app in the **Find people or clubs** box, or by linking to them via Facebook)

7. Click on the **Parties** button to create a group of multiplayer gamers, who can all play together

8. Click on the **Messages** button to send messages to people in your groups and clubs, and also view messages you have received

9. Click on the **Activity alerts** button to view any activity in relation to messages you have sent or comments you have made

9 Microsoft Edge Browser

The Microsoft Edge browser is fast and responsive, and has a range of impressive features. This chapter looks at how to use the Edge browser to open web pages, use tabs, bookmark pages and create Collections of your favorite web items within a single panel.

About the Edge Browser

The web browser Internet Explorer (IE) has been synonymous with Microsoft for almost as long as the Windows operating system. Introduced in 1995, shortly after Windows 95, it was the default browser for a generation of web users. However, as with most technologies, the relentless march of time caught up with IE and it has been superseded by a web browser designed specifically for the digital mobile age. It is called Microsoft Edge, and adapts easily to whichever environment it is operating in: desktop, tablet or phone.

The Microsoft Edge browser has a number of performance and speed enhancements compared with IE, and it also recognizes that modern web users want a lot more from their browser than simply being able to look at web pages.

There is also an option for creating Collections, which is a panel where you can store a range of items, including web pages and photos, related to a similar subject.

Click on this icon from the **Taskbar** or the **Start** menu to open the Microsoft Edge browser at the default Start page:

The Edge browser has been updated in Windows 11, with a redesigned interface and a number of new features.

For details about connecting to a network, and the internet, see pages 207-208.

Click on the **Settings** button in the top right-hand corner of the Microsoft Edge Homepage to access page layout options.

The Start page can be replaced by your own specific Homepage – see page 180 for details.

178

Tab management   Refresh   New tab   Favorites   Collections

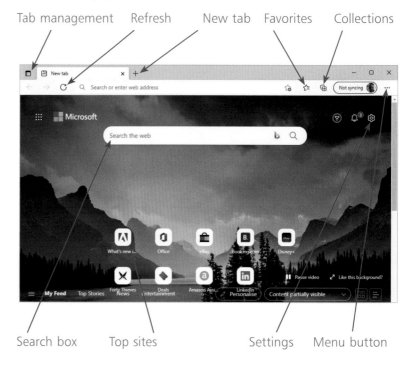

Search box   Top sites   Settings   Menu button

Smart Address Bar

Smart address bars are now a familiar feature in a lot of modern browsers, and Microsoft Edge is no different. This can be used to enter a specific web address to open that page or use it to search for a word or phrase. To use the smart address bar:

1 Click anywhere in the address box at the top of a web page

Hot tip

The personal digital assistant, Cortana, can also be used to open web pages, by asking it to open a specific page. The page will be opened in Microsoft Edge.

2 Start typing a word or website address. As you type, options appear below the address bar. Click on a web page address to open that website

3 Click on one of the options to view the search result for that item

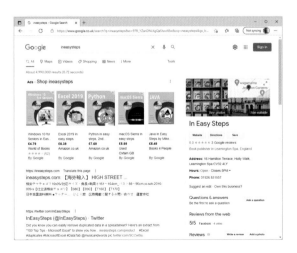

A full list of the Edge settings is displayed in the left-hand sidebar. If this is not showing, click on this button at the top of the Settings window:

Within the settings for Microsoft Edge there is an option for importing Favorites from another web browser. To do this, select **Settings** > **Profiles** > **Import browser data** and click on the **Choose what to import** button to access options for items you want to import.

Setting a Homepage

By default, the Edge browser opens at a web page determined by Windows. However, it is possible to set your own Homepage that is available whenever you open the Edge browser. To do this:

1 Click on this button on the top toolbar to access the menu options

2 Click on the **Settings** button

3 Click on the **Start, home, and new tabs** button in the left-hand sidebar

| Start, home, and new tabs

4 In the **When Microsoft Edge starts** section, check **On** the **Open these pages** option

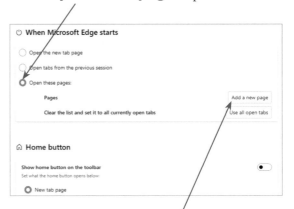

5 Click on the **Add a new page** button

6 Enter the web address (URL) for the required page and click on the **Add** button

Using Tabs

Being able to open several web pages at the same time in different tabs is a standard feature in most web browsers. To do this with Microsoft Edge:

1 Click on this button at the top of the Microsoft Edge window

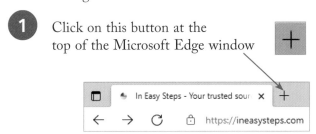

The Start page for new tabs, as displayed in Step 2, can be changed if required. To do this, open the Microsoft Edge settings and access the **Start, home, and new tabs** section as shown in Step 3 on the previous page. Check **On** the **Open the new tabs page** heading and select a page in the same way as for selecting a Homepage.

2 Pages can be opened in new tabs using the smart address bar or from the news items in **My Feed**, **Top Stories** or other news categories that appear below it

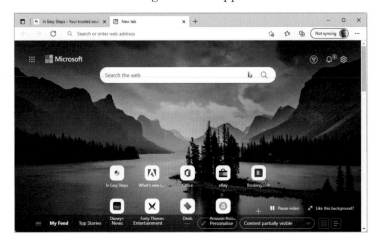

3 All open tabs are displayed at the top of the window. Click and hold on a tab to drag it into a new position

Managing Tabs

Once tabs have been opened in the Edge browser there are a number of options for viewing and managing them.

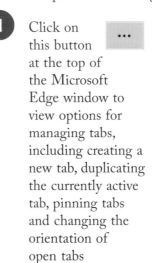

The options for managing tabs in the Edge browser have been updated in Windows 11.

1 Click on this button at the top of the Microsoft Edge window to view options for managing tabs, including creating a new tab, duplicating the currently active tab, pinning tabs and changing the orientation of open tabs

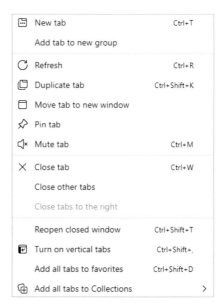

New tab		Ctrl+T
Add tab to new group		
Refresh		Ctrl+R
Duplicate tab		Ctrl+Shift+K
Move tab to new window		
Pin tab		
Mute tab		Ctrl+M
Close tab		Ctrl+W
Close other tabs		
Close tabs to the right		
Reopen closed window		Ctrl+Shift+T
Turn on vertical tabs		Ctrl+Shift+,
Add all tabs to favorites		Ctrl+Shift+D
Add all tabs to Collections		>

2 Click on this button at the left-hand side of the tab bar to access more options

3 Click on the **Turn on vertical tabs** option to change the orientation of the tab bar

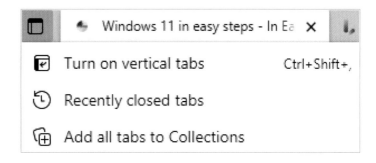

Click on the **Add all tabs to Collections** option in Step 3 to add all of the open tabs to a Collection. See pages 186-187 for details about using Collections.

4 The tab bar is displayed down the left-hand side of the Edge browser window

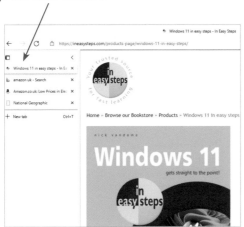

Using vertical tabs is a new feature in Windows 11.

5 Click on this button in Step 4 to minimize the vertical tab bar

6 Click on this button to expand the minimized tab bar

The vertical tabs option can be used even if there is only one open tab.

7 Move the cursor over the minimized tab bar and click on this button to expand it and keep the maximized option in place

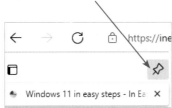

Bookmarking Web Pages

Your favorite web pages can be bookmarked so that you can access them with one click from the **Favorites** button, rather than having to enter the web address each time. To do this:

1 Open the web page that you want to bookmark

2 Click on this button on the toolbar

3 Enter a name for the favorite and where you want it to be saved to

Favorite added

Name   In Easy Steps – Your trusted source for fast

Folder   📁 Favorites bar ⌄

More   Done   Remove

4 Click on the **Done** button   Done

5 The star button turns blue, indicating that the web page has been added as a favorite   ⭐

6 Click on this button to access your favorites (see the next page)   ☆≡

Hot tip

New folders can be created for storing favorites, by clicking in the **Folder** box in Step 4 and clicking on the **New folder** option. The new folder can then be given a new name.

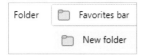

Folder   📁 Favorites bar
          📁 New folder

184

Viewing Favorites

Once pages have been bookmarked in the Edge browser they can be viewed from the **Favorites** button. To do this:

1 Click on this button on the Edge toolbar

2 Click here to view items within the Favorites bar, or other folders that have been created. Click on a bookmarked page to open it

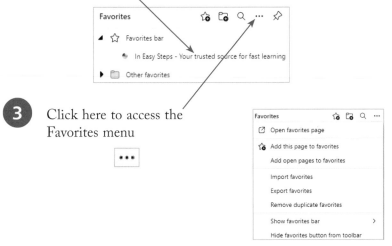

3 Click here to access the Favorites menu

Hot tip

The Favorites bar can also be displayed below the Address bar by opening the Microsoft Edge settings (see page 180) and selecting the **Appearance** option in the left-hand sidebar. In the **Customize toolbar** section, click on the **Show favorites bar** box and select **Always**.

4 Click on the **Show favorites bar** option and select how the Favorites bar is displayed: **Always**, **Never**, or **Only on new tabs**

5 The Favorites bar is displayed below the Address bar

Collections

Collections within the Edge browser is a feature that can be used to store a range of items, including web pages, notes and images. These can then be accessed within the same panel, so that all related items are together. To create collections:

Collections in the Edge browser is a new feature in Windows 11.

1 Right-click on the web page that you are currently viewing and click on the **Add page to Collections** option

2 Click on the **+ Start new collection** button

3 The page is added to a new collection

4 To view collections, click on this button on the Edge toolbar

5 The content of the collection is displayed

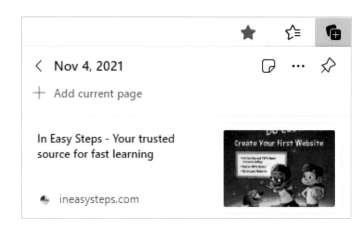

6 Click on the name at the top of the Collections window, and overtype it to give the collection a specific name

7 To add more items to a collection, such as an image, right-click on the item, click on the **Add to Collections** option and select the collection into which it is to be added

8 All of the items within a collection can be viewed in the Collections panel. Click on an item to open it within the Edge browser

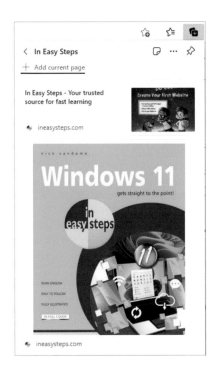

Hot tip

Click on the **Collections** button on the Edge toolbar and click on the **+ Start new collection** option to create another Collection.

Edge Bar

The Edge bar can be used as a free-floating panel that can be kept on-screen at all times to display useful real-time information, such as news stories and weather reports. To use this:

The Edge bar in the Edge browser is a new feature in Windows 11.

1 Click on this button in the top right-hand corner of the Edge browser

···

2 Click on the **More tools** button

More tools

3 Click on the **Launch Edge bar** button

Launch Edge bar

4 The Edge bar is displayed. This can be moved around the screen by clicking and holding here and dragging the panel into the required position

Click on the **Settings** button at the top of the Edge bar window to access its settings.

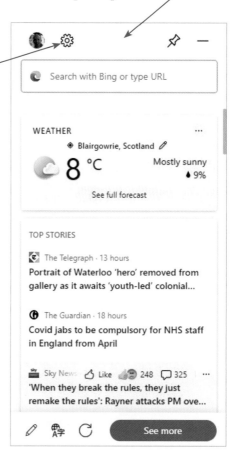

Click on the pin icon at the top of the Edge bar window to pin items within the Edge bar, such as a calendar.

Edge Taskbar

Web pages from the Edge browser can be pinned to the Taskbar so that they can be accessed from here in one click. To do this:

1 Click on this button in the top right-hand corner of the Edge browser

2 Click on the **More tools** button

More tools

3 Click on the **Launch taskbar pinning wizard** button

Launch taskbar pinning wizard

4 Suggested web pages for displaying on the Taskbar are displayed. Select pages as required and click on the **Continue** button

5 Apps from the Edge browser can also be pinned to the Taskbar. Select as required and click on the **Continue** button

6 Click on the **Finish** button

Finish

7 Items selected in Steps 4 and 5 are added to the Taskbar and can be accessed directly from here, by clicking on them

The Edge Taskbar in the Edge browser is a new feature in Windows 11.

Items that have been pinned to the Taskbar with the Taskbar pinning wizard can be removed by right-clicking on them on the Taskbar and clicking on **Unpin from taskbar**.

More Options

There is no traditional Menu bar in Microsoft Edge, but more options can be accessed from the right-hand toolbar.

1 Click on this button to access the menu options

2 Click here to open a new browsing window, or a **New InPrivate window** that does not record any of your browsing history

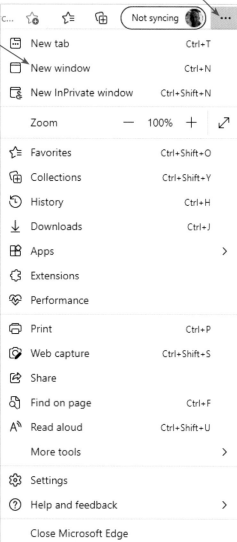

3 Click on the **Zoom** button to increase or decrease the magnification of the page being viewed

4 Click on the **Find on page** button to search for a specific word or phrase on the web page

5 Click on the **Print** button to print the current web page

Don't forget

Click on the **Share** button to send someone a link to the current web page being viewed. This can be done using email, text messaging or social media apps.

10 Keeping in Touch

This chapter looks at keeping in touch with family and friends with the Mail, Chat, People and Calendar apps.

Setting Up Mail

Email has become an essential part of everyday life, both socially and in the business world. Windows 11 accommodates this with the Mail app. This can be used to link to online services such as Gmail and Outlook (the renamed version of Hotmail), and also other email accounts. To set up an email account with Mail:

1 Click on the **Mail** app on the Start menu

2 Click on the **Accounts** button

3 Click on the **Add account** button

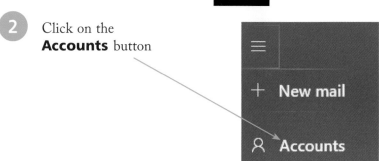

Hot tip

The **Other account** option in Step 4 can be used to add a non-webmail account. This is usually a POP3 or an IMAP account, and you will need your email address, username, password, and usually the incoming and outgoing email servers. If you do not know these, they should be supplied by your email provider. They should also be available in the account settings of the email account you want to add to the Mail app.

4 Select the type of account to which you want to link via the Mail app. This can be an online email account that you have already set up

5 Enter your current sign-in details for the selected email account and click on the **Sign in** button

6 Once it has been connected, details of the account are shown under the **Mail** button, including the mailboxes within the account. Click on the **Accounts** button to view all linked accounts

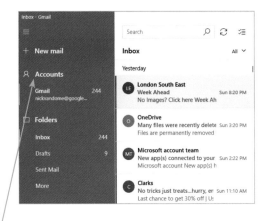

7 A list of emails appears in the middle panel. Double-click on an email to view it at full size

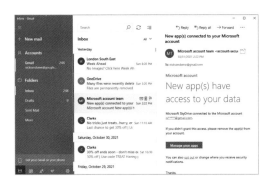

You can add more than one account to the Mail app. If you do this, you will be able to select different accounts to view within Mail.

Click on this button at the top of the left-hand toolbar to expand and collapse menu items, with their text descriptions:

Working with Mail

Once you have set up an account in the Mail app you can then start creating and managing your emails with it.

1 On the main mail page, open an email and click on the **Reply**, **Reply all** or **Forward** buttons to respond

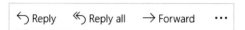

2 Open an email and click on the **Delete** button to remove it

Composing an email
To compose and send an email message:

1 Click on this button to create a new message

2 Click in the **To:** field and enter an email address

194

3 Click on the **Cc & Bcc** link to access options for copying and blind copying

4 The email address can either be in the format of myname@email.com or you can enter the name of one of your contacts from the People app (see pages 200-201), and the email address will be entered automatically

5 Enter a subject heading and body text to the email

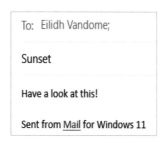

6 Click on the **Insert** button on the top toolbar in the new email window and select one of the options, such as **Pictures**

7 Click on a folder from which you want to attach a file, and click on the **Insert** button

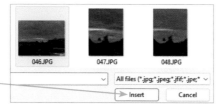

When composing an email, or at any other time, press the Windows key (WinKey) and the period/full stop key on the keyboard to access a panel for adding emojis (graphical symbols) to an item. This can also be used with other messaging apps.

8 The file is shown in the body of the email

9 Select an item of text and select the text formatting options from the top toolbar

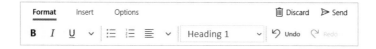

10 Click on this button to send the email

195

Chat App

Windows 11 is integrated closely with the collaboration and communication app Microsoft Teams. Part of this is the Chat app, which is a new feature in Windows 11 and provides text and video chat functions, linked to Microsoft Teams, but provided through an independent app. To get started with Chat:

The Chat app is a new feature in Windows 11.

1 Click on the **Chat** icon on the Taskbar

If the Microsoft Teams app has already been accessed, some of the initial steps for setting up the Chat app may not be required.

2 Click on the **Get started** button

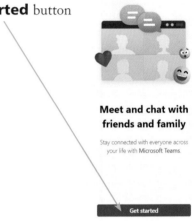

Meet and chat with friends and family

Stay connected with everyone across your life with **Microsoft Teams**.

Get started

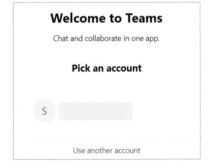

For a detailed look at Microsoft Teams, see **Microsoft Teams in easy steps**.

3 Select the Microsoft Account to use with the Chat app (which links to the parent app, Microsoft Teams). The Microsoft Account is usually the one you use for signing in with Windows 11

Welcome to Teams

Chat and collaborate in one app.

Pick an account

S

Use another account

4 Enter the name you want to appear in the Chat app and click on the **Next** button

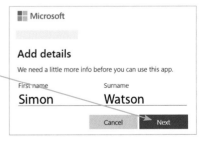

Microsoft

Add details

We need a little more info before you can use this app.

First name — Simon Surname — Watson

Cancel   Next

196

5 Click on the **Let's go** button

6 Click on the **Sync contacts** button to synchronize your contacts from other apps and locations

The Microsoft Teams app has replaced Skype as the default collaboration and communication app within Windows.

7 Click on the options for synchronizing contacts. These will then be available in the Chat app

8 Click on the **Chat** app again to access it, ready for text, audio or video chats. Enter a name in the **To:** box to select someone for a conversation

...cont'd

The **Format** icon in Step 9 includes options for adding bold, italics, underlining, font color and font size. Format selection can be made before text is added, or to selected text.

9 Click in the text box to enter text for the message

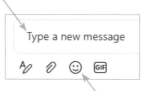

10 Use the icons below the text box to add a range of content to the message; see the next four steps

11 Click on the **Attach Files** button in Step 8 on page 197 and click on the **Upload from my computer** option to select files from your own computer

12 Click on the **Emoji** button in Step 8 on page 197 and click on an emoji to add it to the text message

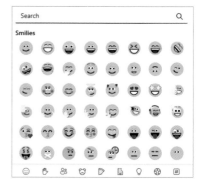

13 Scroll down the emoji page, or click on the toolbar at the bottom of the panel, to access different categories of emojis

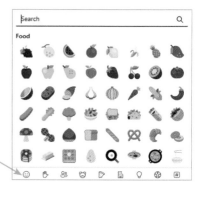

14 Click on the **GIF** button in Step 9 on the previous page to access animated and graphical GIF images. Click on a GIF to add it to the text message

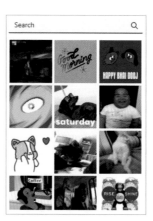

15 A conversation is created within the chat window and continues down the window as more content is added

16 Click on this button to send a text message

17 Use these buttons in the top right-hand corner of the chat box to, from left to right: start a video call with the person in the conversation; start an audio call with the person in the conversation; and add people for text, video or audio calls

Don't forget

Click on this button in Step 16 and enter the details of a new contact, to add someone to the conversation:

Finding People

An electronic address book is always a good feature to have on a computer, and with Windows 11 this function is provided by the People app. This not only allows you to add your own contacts manually; you can also link to any of your online accounts, such as Gmail or iCloud, and import the contacts that you have there. In Windows 11, the People app is accessed from the Mail app.

Don't forget

If the People app is being used for the first time there will be a page with an option to add contacts from an existing account, such as Google or iCloud. If an account has already been added for the Mail app then this can be used, and there is also an **Import contacts** option for importing from another account.

Hot tip

You can also select accounts to add to the People app from the Homepage when you first open it.

Hot tip

To delete a contact, right-click on their name in the Contacts list and click on the **Delete** button to remove them.

1 Open the Mail app and click on this button in the bottom left-hand corner

2 The current contacts are displayed. Double-click on a contact to view their details

3 Click on a letter at the top of a section to access the alpha search list. Click on a letter to view contacts starting with the selected letter

4 Click on the **Settings** button to add new accounts from which you want to import contacts, such as a Gmail or an iCloud account (in the same way as setting up a new email account). Click on the **+ Add an account** button to add the required account. The contacts from the linked account are imported to the People app

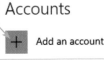

200

Adding contacts manually

As well as importing contacts, it is also possible to enter them manually into the People app.

1 Click on the **New contact** button on the top toolbar

2 Enter details for the new contact, including name, email address and phone number

Hot tip

Once a contact has been added, select it as in Step 2 on the previous page and click on this button to edit the contact's details:

3 Click on the Down arrow next to a field to access additional options for that item

Hot tip

When a contact has been selected, click on the pin icon on the top toolbar and select either **Pin to Taskbar** or **Pin to Start** to pin the contact here. More than three contacts can now be pinned in this way.

4 Click on the **Save** button at the bottom of the window to create a new contact

Using the Calendar

The Calendar app can be used to record important events and reminders. To view the calendar:

1 Click on the **Calendar** app on the Start menu

2 Click here to view the calendar in **Day**, **Week**, or **Month** mode

Accounts can be added to the Calendar app in the same way as for the Mail and People apps.

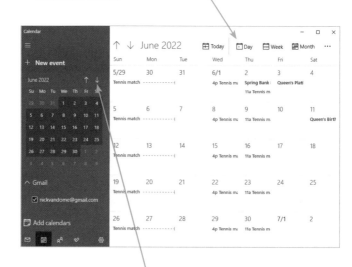

Click on the **Week** option in Step 2 to access options for displaying the calendar as a **Work week** – i.e. five days (Monday to Friday) – or a full **Week**.

3 Click on these buttons to move between months (or swipe left or right on a touchpad)

Adding events

Events can be added to the calendar and various settings can be applied to them, such as recurrence and reminders.

1. Click on a date to create a new event and click on the **+ New event** button

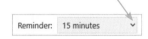

2. Enter an **Event name** and a **Location** at the top of the window

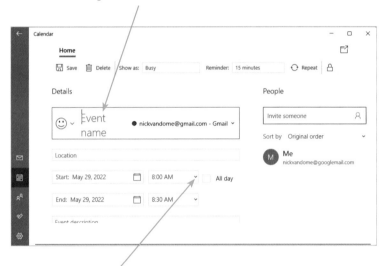

3. Click here and select a time for the start and end of the event

4. If **All day** is selected, the time fields will not be available

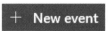

...cont'd

5 For a recurring event, click on the **Repeat** button at the top of the window

6 Select an option for the recurrence, such as **Weekly**

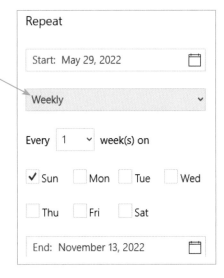

When an event is due, an alert will appear on the screen.

7 Click on the **Save** button to save an event to the calendar, or click on the **Delete** button to remove it

8 To delete an existing event or series of events (i.e. one that has repeat occurrences), right-click on it and click on the **Delete** button

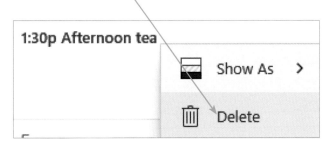

11 Networking and Sharing

Windows 11 has a
built-in networking
capability, for connecting
to the internet and also
sharing files between two
(or more) computers.

Network Components

There are numerous possibilities for setting up a home network. To start with, there are two major network technologies:

- **Wireless** – using radio waves to send data at rates of 11 to 300 Mbps (megabits per second) or up to – in theory – 1 Gbps (gigabit per second) with the latest devices (although all of these are theoretical top speeds).

- **Wired** – e.g. Ethernet, using twisted pair cables to send data at rates of 10, 100 or 1,000 Mbps.

There is also a variety of hardware items required:

- **Network adapter** – appropriate to the network type, with one for each computer in the network.

- **Network controller** – one or more hub, switch or router, providing the actual connection to each network adapter.

There is also the internet connection (dial-up, DSL or cable), using:

- A modem connected to one of the computers.

- A modem connected to the network.

- Internet access incorporated into the router or switch.

Setting up the components

The steps you will need, and the most appropriate sequence to follow, will depend on the specific options on your system. However, the main steps will include:

- Install network adapters in the computers, where necessary (in most cases these will be pre-installed in the computer).

- Set up or verify the internet connection – this should be provided by your Internet Service Provider (ISP).

- Configure the wireless router or access point – this could involve installing software for the router, which may be provided on a CD or DVD. (Some routers will be automatically recognized by Windows 11.)

- Start up Windows on your PC.

Windows 11 is designed to automate as much of the network setup task as possible.

A network adapter can be connected to the USB port, inserted in the PC card slot or installed inside your computer.

Ethernet adapters connect to a network hub, switch or wired router. Wireless adapters connect through a wireless router or a combination of router/switch.

You may already have some of these elements in operation, if you have an existing network running a previous version of Windows.

Connecting to a Network

You can connect your computers to form a network using Ethernet cables and adapters, or by setting up wireless adapters and routers. When you start up each computer, Windows 11 will examine the current configuration and discover any new networks that have been established since the last start-up. You can check this, or connect manually to a network, from within the Wi-Fi settings from the Network & internet section of Settings. To do this:

1 Open the **Settings** app and click on the **Network & internet** tab

2 With no network currently connected, drag the **Wi-Fi** button **On**

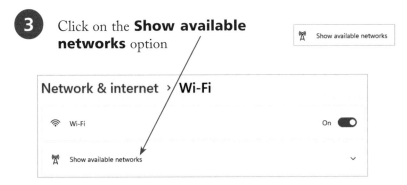

3 Click on the **Show available networks** option

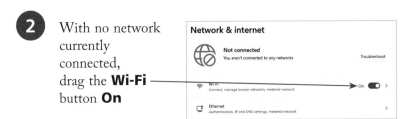

4 Click on the required network

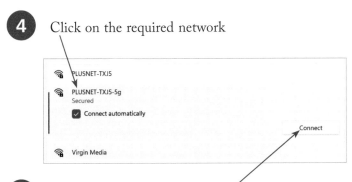

5 Click on the **Connect** button

Beware

The most common type of network for connecting to is the internet.

Beware

If your network is unavailable for any reason, this will be noted in Step 2.

...cont'd

6 Enter the password for the router to be used to connect to the Wi-Fi network

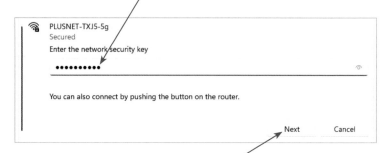

7 Click on the **Next** button

8 If the connection is successful, the network name is shown as **Connected**

9 Connected networks are shown at the top of the Network & internet settings window

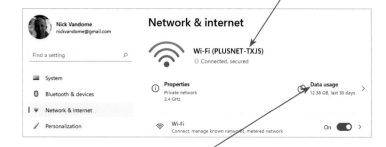

10 Click on the **Data usage** button to see which apps are using the most data on the network

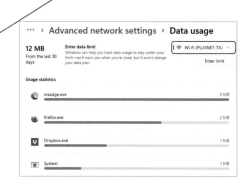

Viewing Network Status

Once you have connected to a network, and usually the internet too, you can view your current network status. To do this:

1 From the main Network & internet settings page, click on the **Properties** button for the connected network

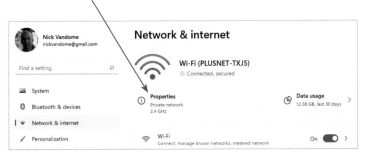

2 Check **On** either the **Public network** or the **Private network** option to hide your device on the network (Public network) or make it discoverable for sharing items with other people (Private network)

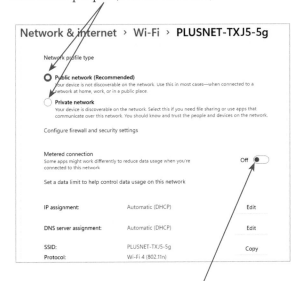

3 Drag the **Metered connection** button **Off** to reduce the amount of data that is processed across the network, if you have a limited data Wi-Fi service (Windows applies the required settings for reducing the data usage)

Don't forget

Click on the **Advanced network settings** option on the main Network & internet page to view details about the elements that make up networks in Windows 11.

Advanced network settings
View all network adapters, network reset

Nearby Sharing

Nearby sharing can be used to share files wirelessly, either using Bluetooth or Wi-Fi. As the name suggests, the computer with which you want to share files has to be relatively close to the one that is sharing the content. Also, the other device has to support Nearby sharing; i.e. be running a compatible version of Windows 11. To use Nearby sharing:

1 Open the **Settings** app and click on the **System** tab

2 Click on the **Nearby sharing** option

3 Click here in the **Nearby sharing** option

If your PC does not have Wi-Fi or Bluetooth capability, the **Nearby sharing** option will not be available.

210

4 Select who you want to be able to share content with your computer. It can be everyone, or only your own devices; i.e. ones on which you have signed in with your Microsoft Account details

5 Under the **Save files I receive to** heading, in Step 3 on the previous page, click on the **Change** button to select a new location

6 Select a new location for files that are shared with Nearby sharing and click on the **Select Folder** button

Sharing files

Once Nearby sharing has been set up it can be used to share files wirelessly with other compatible devices. To do this:

1 Open File Explorer and select a file. Click on the **Share** button on the Menu bar

Both devices have to be set up for **Nearby sharing** for it to work effectively.

2 Select an option for sharing the item with someone else, including **Nearby sharing**, as shown on the previous page. Items can also be shared via email, social media and online storage apps

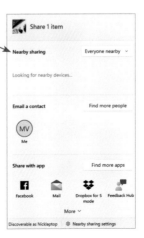

Sharing Settings

Options for specifying how items are shared over a network can be selected in the Network and Sharing Center. To access these (from the Settings app):

1 Open the **Settings** app, enter "**sharing settings**" into the Search box and click on the **Manage advanced sharing settings** option

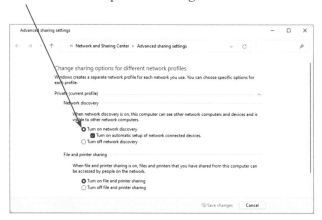

2 Select sharing options for different networks, including **Private**, **Guest or Public**, and **All** networks. Options can be selected for turning on network discovery so that your computer can see other computers on the network, and for file and printer sharing

If you are sharing over a network you should be able to access the Public folder on another computer (providing that network discovery is turned on). If you are the administrator of the other computer you will also be able to access your own Home folder, although you will need to enter the required password for this.

3 Click on these arrowheads to expand the options for each network category

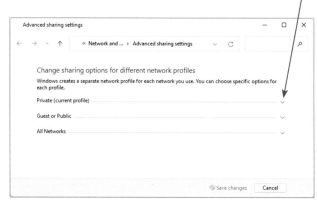

Viewing Network Components

You can also view the components of the network in File Explorer. To do this:

1 Open File Explorer and click on the **Network** Library, to view items within the network

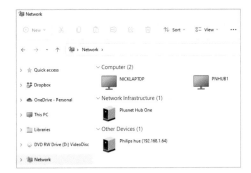

2 To view the shared items offered by a particular computer (for example, NICKLAPTOP), double-click on the associated icon

The Public folder on your own computer can be used to make items available to other users on the network.

3 Double-click to view the contents of networked folders

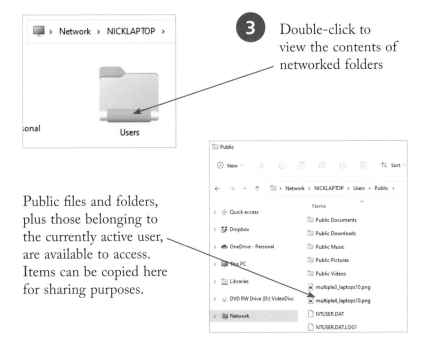

Public files and folders, plus those belonging to the currently active user, are available to access. Items can be copied here for sharing purposes.

Network Troubleshooting

1 Open the **Settings** app, enter "**network troubleshoot**" into the Search box and click on the **Find and fix network problems** option

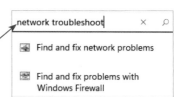

For more Windows 11 troubleshooting options, see page 218-219.

2 Click on the option that most closely matches your network problem

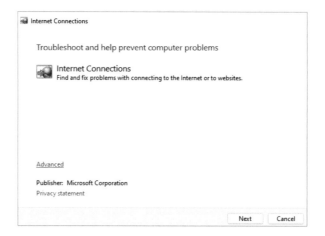

3 Most options have additional selections that can be made to try to solve the problem. Click on these as required

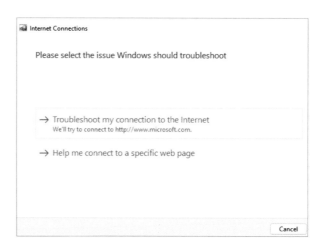

12 System and Security

Windows 11 includes tools to help protect your online privacy, troubleshoot common problems, maintain your hard drive, protect against malicious software, and back up your content.

Privacy

Online privacy is a major issue for all computer users, and Windows 11 has a number of options for viewing details about your personal online privacy.

The Privacy options have been updated in Windows 11.

1 Open the **Settings** app and click on the **Privacy & security** tab

2 The Privacy & security options are displayed in the **Security** and **Windows permissions** sections (and the **App permissions** section further down the page; see Step 7 on the next page)

3 Click on the **General** items under the **Windows permissions** heading to select options for: allowing, or denying, advertising more specific to you; letting websites provide local advertising content based on the language used within Windows; letting Windows track your app usage for improving the Start menu and search results; and showing specific results within the Settings app

Click on **Privacy Statement** in Step 3 to view Microsoft's privacy statement (this is an online statement and, by default, is displayed within the Edge browser).

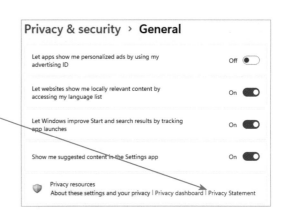

4 Click on the **Search permissions** option under the **Windows permissions** heading shown in Step 2 on the previous page

Search permissions
SafeSearch, cloud content search, search history

5 Select options for **SafeSearch**, to specify the type of content that can be displayed from web searches →

Privacy & security › **Search permissions**

To give you relevant results, Windows Search will search the web, apps, settings, and files. To change which files on your device are searched, go to Searching Windows

SafeSearch

In Windows Search, web previews will not automatically load web results if they may contain adult content. If you choose to preview web results, we'll apply the following setting:

○ Strict — Filter out adult text, images, and videos from my web results

● Moderate — Filter adult images and videos but not text from my web results

○ Off — Don't filter adult content from my web results

Hot tip

If **Find my device** is turned **On**, the device can be located on the web. To do this, log in to your Microsoft Account at account.microsoft.com

6 Under the **Security** section, select options for: **Windows Security**; **Find my device**, for locating a missing Windows 11 device; and **For developers**, for advanced users

Security

🛡 Windows Security
Antivirus, browser, firewall, and network protection for your device

👤 Find my device
Track your device if you think you've lost it

🛠 For developers
These settings are intended for development use only

7 Under the **App permissions** section, click on specific apps to set their own options for security and permissions

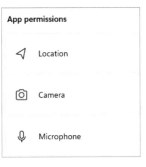

App permissions

◁ Location

📷 Camera

🎤 Microphone

The Troubleshooting options have been updated in Windows 11.

The **Recommended troubleshooter preferences** include a range of options that are selected automatically by Windows 11.

Troubleshooting

On any computing system there are always things that go wrong or do not work properly. Windows 11 is no different, but there are comprehensive troubleshooting options for trying to address a range of problems. To use these:

1 Open the **Settings** app, select **System** and click on the **Troubleshoot** option

2 Recommended troubleshooting options are displayed within the main window

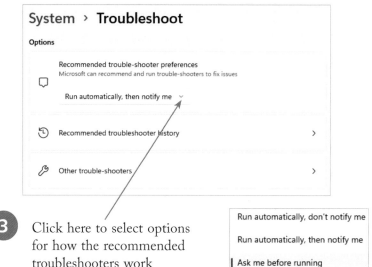

3 Click here to select options for how the recommended troubleshooters work

Run automatically, don't notify me

Run automatically, then notify me

Ask me before running

Don't run any

4 Click on the **Recommended troubleshooter history** button in Step 2 to view the most recent troubleshooters that have been run

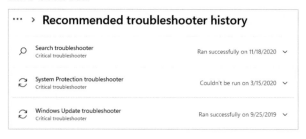

5 Click on the **Other trouble-shooters** button in Step 2 on the previous page to access troubleshooting options for specific hardware items and apps

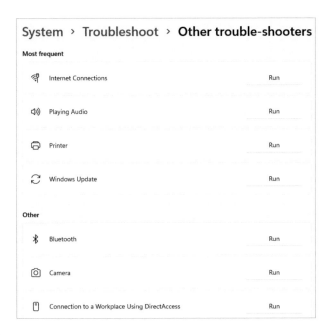

Try the troubleshooting options first for hardware devices before you try to physically repair any problems.

6 Click on one of the categories to select it, and click on the **Run** button

7 The troubleshooting process will run for the selected item and a report is displayed once the troubleshooting has been completed. Click on the **Close** button

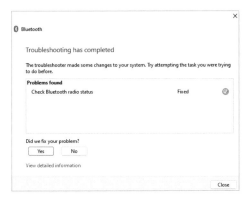

System Properties

There are several ways to open the System properties, and view information about your computer:

- Select **Settings** > **System** > **About**; or

- Press the **WinKey** + the **Pause/Break** keys; or

- Right-click **This PC** in the File Explorer Navigation pane, then select **Properties** from the menu

Device Manager

1 Right-click on the **Start** button and click on the **Device Manager** option from the menu

Device Manager

2 Select the > symbol to expand that entry to show details

3 Double-click any device to open its properties

The main System panel (About) provides the Windows 11 edition, processor details, memory size and device name.

You may be prompted for an administrator password or asked for permission to continue when you select some Device Manager entries.

4 Select the Driver tab and select **Update Driver** to find and install new software

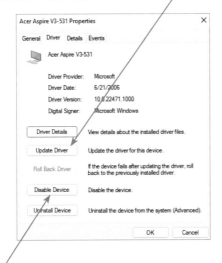

Click on the **Roll Back Driver** button (if available) to switch back to the previously installed driver for a device if the new one for it fails.

5 Select **Disable Device** to put the particular device offline. The button changes to **Enable Device**, to reverse the action

Enable Device

Cleaning Up Your Disk

The Cleanup options within the Settings app can be used to remove items on your computer that are no longer required, thus freeing up more space on your hard drive. To use these:

1 In Settings, select **System** > **Storage** and click on the **Cleanup recommendations** option

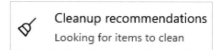

The Cleanup options have been updated in Windows 11.

2 Check **On** any items that you are happy about removing from your computer; e.g. the contents of the **Recycle Bin**

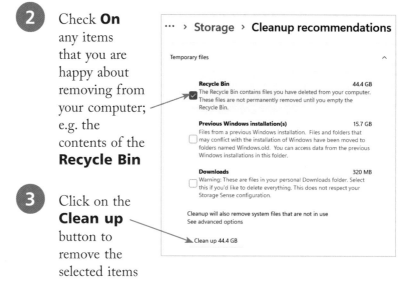

3 Click on the **Clean up** button to remove the selected items

If the Recycle Bin option is selected in Step 2, the items contained within it will be deleted permanently and will not be able to be restored.

4 Scroll down the page to select particularly large or unused files. Select them in the same way as in Step 2 and click on the **Clean up** button to remove them

Clean up 17.5 MB

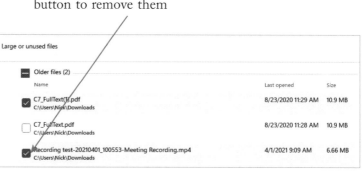

...cont'd

When a file is written to the hard disk, it may be stored in several pieces in different places. This fragmentation of disk space can slow down your computer. Disk Defragmenter rearranges the data so that the disk will work more efficiently.

1 In File Explorer, right-click on the **C:** drive and click on the **Properties** option

Spellings are localized.

2 Select the **Tools** tab and click on the **Optimize** button

3 The process runs as a scheduled task, but you can select a drive and select **Analyze** to check out a new drive

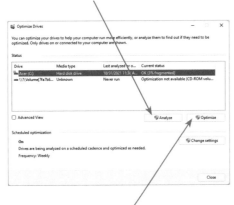

Only disks that can be fragmented are shown. These can include USB drives that you add to your system.

4 Click the **Optimize** button to process the selected disk drive. This may take between several minutes to several hours to complete, depending on the size and state of the disk, but you can still use your computer while the task is running

Windows Update

Updates to Windows 11 and other Microsoft products are supplied regularly to help prevent or fix problems, improve security or enhance performance. The way in which they are downloaded and installed can be specified from the Settings app.

If there are no updates displayed in Step 2, click on the **Check for updates** button.

1 Open the **Settings** app and click on the **Windows Update** tab

2 There are a range of options available on the main Windows Update page, for managing the way that updates are performed on your PC or laptop

If there are updates displayed in Step 2, click on the **Download now** button.

An icon for alerting you to available updates can be placed on the Taskbar, rather than having to check within the Settings app each time. To set this up, access **Settings** > **Windows Update** > **Advanced options** and drag **On** the **Notify me when a restart is required to finish updating** option. When an update is available, the icon on the Taskbar will display an orange dot.

3 Click on the **Pause for 1 week** option to stop updates being installed for seven days

4 A yellow icon appears on the Windows Update page, indicating that updates have been paused. Click on the **Resume updates** button to resume them again

224

5 Click on the **Update history** button

6 The Windows update history is displayed, with the most recent updates at the top of the list

7 Click on the **Advanced options** button

8 The Advanced options include options for specifying if you receive updates about Microsoft products other than Windows 11, and for receiving notifications about restarts following an update

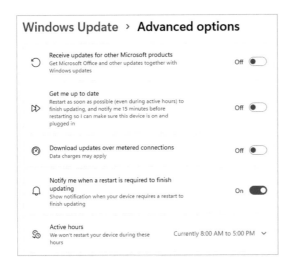

Drag the **Get me up to date** button **On** in Step 8 to ensure that once updates have been installed, the computer will restart as soon as possible afterward, to complete the update. A notification will be sent 15 minutes before the restart is due.

...cont'd

9 Scroll down the **Advanced options** page to view the **Additional options** section, including **Optional updates**, which can be used for updating drivers for items such as printers, and also options for resetting Windows 11 (**Recovery**)

10 Click on the **Active hours** option in Step 8 on page 225

11 Select times during which your computer won't be restarted, if an update has been installed automatically (to prevent it from restarting when you are using it)

12 Click on the **Windows Insider Program** button in Step 2 on page 224 to set up options for receiving preview copies of Windows, before a general release

Hot tip

If the Windows Insider Program has been activated from the option in Step 11, it can be stopped by clicking on the **Stop getting preview builds** in the Windows Insider Program window.

Backing Up

Backing up your data is an important task in any computer environment, and in Windows 11 this can be done from within the File History section of the Control Panel, which can also be accessed from the Settings app. To do this:

1 Connect an external storage device, such as an external hard drive, to your computer

2 Access the **Settings** app and enter "**file history**" into the Search box and click on **Restore your files with File History**

3 Click **Configure File History settings** then click the **System Image Backup** option in the bottom left-hand corner of the File History window that appears

4 Click on the **Set up backup** option

5 Click on the **Run now** option

6 Select the required external device for the backup and click on the **Next** button to complete the backup

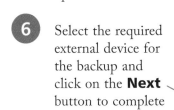

Folders can also be backed up with the OneDrive online storage function. To do this, select **Settings** > **Accounts** > **Windows backup**. Click on the **Set up syncing** button (or **Manage sync settings** button if syncing has already been set up) in the **OneDrive folder syncing** section and select folders to be backed up and synced with OneDrive.

Hot tip

Files and folders can also be backed up by copying them in File Explorer and then pasting them into an external device, such as a USB flashdrive.

System Restore

Windows 11 takes snapshots of system files before any software updates are applied, or in any event once every seven days. You can also create a snapshot manually. The snapshots are known as Restore Points and are managed by System Restore.

1 In Settings, access **System > About** and click on the **Advanced system settings** link

2 Click on the **System Protection** tab and click on the **Create...** button

3 Provide a title for the Restore Point and click **Create**

4 The required data is written to disk and the manual Restore Point is set up

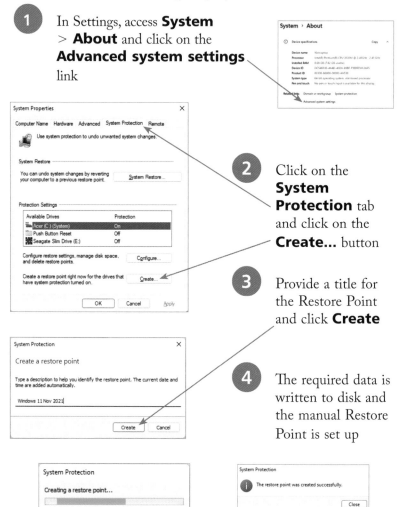

Using Restore Points

The installation of a new app or driver software may make Windows 11 behave unpredictably or have other unexpected results. Usually, uninstalling the app or rolling back the driver (see page 221) will correct the situation. If this does not fix the problem, use an automatic or manual Restore Point to reset your system to an earlier date when everything worked correctly.

1 Select **System Protection** and click the **System Restore...** button

2 By default, this will offer to undo the most recent change. This may fix the problem

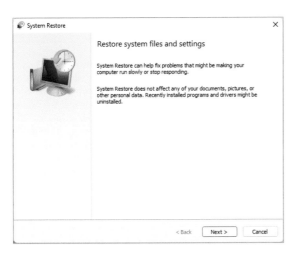

3 Otherwise, click a suitable item to use as the Restore Point

Don't forget

If the selected Restore Point does not resolve the problem, you can try again, selecting another Restore Point.

4 Follow the prompts to restart the system using system files from the selected date and time

Windows Security

The Windows Security app, which is pre-installed with
Windows 11, can be used to give a certain amount of protection
against viruses and malicious software. To use it:

1 Select **Settings** > **Privacy &
security**

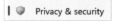

2 Click on the **Windows
Security** option and you'll
see options listed under the
Protection areas heading

Click on the **Virus &
threat protection**
option in Step 2 to run
a virus check over your
computer.

3 Click on
one of the
**Protection
areas**
categories
to view its
options

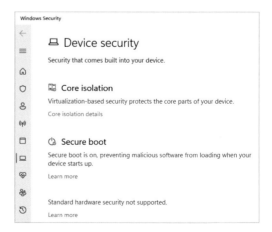

4 Click on the **Open Windows Security** button on the main security page to open the Windows Security app

5 Click each item to view its options and use the left-hand toolbar to move between sections. Click on the **Home** button to return to this page

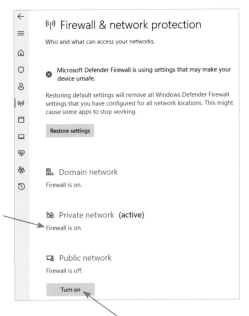

Using a firewall

A firewall can be used to help protect your network from viruses and malicious software. To set this up:

1 Click on the **Firewall & network protection** option on the Windows Security Homepage

2 The related networks are listed, with their firewall status; e.g. **Firewall is on**

3 If a firewall is **Off** for any item, click on the **Turn on** button to activate it

Hot tip

The Microsoft Firewall can be used to provide a level of protection against malicious software and viruses.

Don't forget

Firewall is on by default in Windows 11, but you can turn it off if you have another firewall installed and active.

...cont'd

Protecting against viruses

The Windows Security center can be used to give a certain amount of protection against viruses and malicious software. To do this:

Malware (malicious software) is designed to deliberately harm your computer. To protect your system, you need up-to-date antivirus and anti-spyware software. The Windows Security option provides this, and you can also install a separate antivirus app.

1 On the Windows Security Homepage, click on the **Virus & threat protection** option

Protection areas

Virus & threat protection
Actions recommended.

2 Click on the **Quick scan** button to scan your system for viruses

🛡 Virus & threat protection

Protection for your device against threats.

🕒 **Current threats**

No current threats.
Last scan: 10/6/2021 9:54 AM (quick scan)
0 threat(s) found.
Scan lasted 15 minutes 11 seconds
42526 files scanned.

Quick scan

Scan options

Allowed threats

Protection history

Click on the **Scan options** link in Step 2 to access options for more comprehensive scans over your computer.

Scan options

3 Once the scan is completed, any threats will be noted and options for dealing with them listed; e.g. remove or quarantine an item(s)

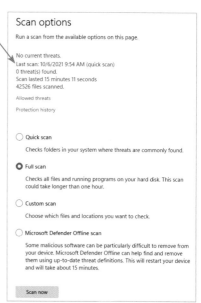

Scan options

Run a scan from the available options on this page.

No current threats.
Last scan: 10/6/2021 9:54 AM (quick scan)
0 threat(s) found.
Scan lasted 15 minutes 11 seconds
42526 files scanned.

Allowed threats

Protection history

○ Quick scan

Checks folders in your system where threats are commonly found.

● Full scan

Checks all files and running programs on your hard disk. This scan could take longer than one hour.

○ Custom scan

Choose which files and locations you want to check.

○ Microsoft Defender Offline scan

Some malicious software can be particularly difficult to remove from your device. Microsoft Defender Offline can help find and remove them using up-to-date threat definitions. This will restart your device and will take about 15 minutes.

Scan now

Index

O

P

N

Q

R

S